THE ZOO STORY
and Other Plays

EDWARD ALBEE

THE
ZOO STORY

and Other Plays

JONATHAN CAPE
THIRTY BEDFORD SQUARE
LONDON

FIRST PUBLISHED IN GREAT BRITAIN 1962
REPRINTED 1969
© 1960 AND 1961 BY EDWARD ALBEE

SBN 224 60005 2

PRINTED IN GREAT BRITAIN BY
WILLIAM LEWIS (PRINTERS) LTD, CARDIFF
ON PAPER MADE BY JOHN DICKINSON & CO. LTD
BOUND BY A. W. BAIN & CO. LTD, LONDON.

CONTENTS

Introduction   7

The American Dream   11

The Death of Bessie Smith   59

The Sandbox   99

The Zoo Story   111

INTRODUCTION

With the exception of a three-act sex farce I composed when I was twelve — the action of which occurred aboard an ocean liner, the characters of which were, for the most part, English gentry, and which either I lost or my mother threw away — with the exception of that, the four plays printed here, *The Zoo Story* (1958), *The Death of Bessie Smith* and *The Sandbox* (both 1959), and *The American Dream* (1960), are my first four plays.

The Zoo Story, written first, received production first — but not in the United States, where one might reasonably expect an American writer to get his first attention. *The Zoo Story* had its première in Berlin, Germany, on September 28th, 1959. How it got to production so shortly after it was written, and how, especially, it got to Berlin, might be of interest — perhaps to point up the Unusual, the Unlikely, the Unexpected, which, with the exception of the fare the commercial theatre set-up spills out on its dogged audience each season, is the nature of the theatre.

Shortly after *The Zoo Story* was completed, and while it was being read and politely refused by a number of New York producers (which was not to be unexpected, for no one at all had ever heard of its author, and it *was* a short play, and short plays *are*, unfortunately, anathema to producers and — supposedly — to audiences), a young composer friend of mine, William Flanagan by name, looked at the play, liked it, and sent it to several friends of his, among them David Diamond, another American composer, resident in Italy; Diamond liked the play and sent it on to a friend of *his*, a Swiss actor, Pinkas Braun; Braun liked the play, made a tape recording of it, playing both its roles, which he sent on to

Mrs Stefani Hunzinger, who heads the drama department of the S. Fischer Verlag, a large publishing house in Frankfurt; she, in turn ... well, through her it got to Berlin, and to production. From New York to Florence to Zurich to Frankfurt to Berlin. And finally back to New York where, on January 14th, 1960, it received American production, off-Broadway, at the Provincetown Playhouse, on a double-bill with Samuel Beckett's *Krapp's Last Tape*.

The Zoo Story has been received enthusiastically wherever it has played — with the exception of London. (This rather surprised me, for it seemed to me that a city which would make equal hits out of so fine a play as Harold Pinter's *The Caretaker* and such dreck as Rattigan's *Ross*, was either an easy mark or friendly to everything.) But London aside, *The Zoo Story* has fared well in Germany, Austria, Holland, Turkey, Israel, Argentina, Uruguay and several other countries, and, too, in the United States, where it played six hundred performances in New York City.

It was a gratifying response to have for a first play.

The Sandbox, which is fourteen minutes long, was written to satisfy a commission from the Festival of Two Worlds for a short dramatic piece for the Festival's summer programme in Spoleto, Italy — where it was not performed. It has found a happy home on United States television on special (unsponsored — thank heavens) programmes, to the horror of television critics, who have found the play incomprehensible.

The Death of Bessie Smith had its première in Berlin, as did *The Zoo Story*, and is, at this writing, enjoying a successful run in New York City, on a double-bill with *The American Dream*.

The circumstances surrounding the death of Bessie Smith, the Negro blues singer, provided the initial stimulus for the play; and perhaps a very fine play — a great deal better than

8

mine, it is not unlikely — could be contrived from nothing more than the facts of that ugly episode; but while I was getting the thing to mind and (concurrently) to paper, while the incident, itself, was brawling at me, and while the characters I had elected to carry the tale were wresting it from me, I discovered that I was, in fact, writing about something at the same time slightly removed from and more pertinent to what I had imagined. I do not know whether this while-working alteration/amplification of the genetic matter has resulted in a better play than I had at first conceived, or whether, in its final form, the piece is only diffuse and directionless. I know only that the play, printed here, is, whatever its failings or successes may be, most exactly what I had to say on the matter.

About *The American Dream* I find there is very little to say. It has in it several characters from *The Sandbox*, though it is not merely an extension of that play. Its opening moments owe a great debt to Ionesco's *The Bald Soprano*, but the rest is me; it has been, I think, received the best of my four plays in New York, and I am still too close to having written it to have any feelings about it other than great fondness.

EDWARD ALBEE

New York City
  August 30th, 1961

THE AMERICAN DREAM

A Play in One Scene (1959–1960)

for
DAVID DIAMOND

FIRST PERFORMANCE: January 24th, 1961. New York City.
York Playhouse.

PREFACE

Some favourable comments printed on the jacket of the American edition of this play, while they are representative of a majority of American critical reaction to the play, do not tell the whole story. Naturally not. No sensible publisher will tout opinions antagonistic to his product. And while I have in my brief (three years, five plays – two of them but fifteen minutes long) and happy time as a playwright, received enough good press to last me a lifetime, I would like to concern myself, here, with some of the bad – not because I am a masochist, but because I would like to point up, foolhardy though it may be of me, what I consider to be a misuse of the critical function in American press letters.

For example: The off-Broadway critic for one of New York's morning tabloids had his sensibilities (or something) so offended by the *content* of *The American Dream* that he refused to review the next play of mine that opened.

Another example: A couple of other critics (Bright Gentlemen who do their opinions for Intellectualist Weekly Sheets of – sadly, all in all – very small circulation) went all to pieces over the (to their mind) nihilist, immoral, defeatist *content* of the play. And so on.

May I submit that when a critic sets himself up as an arbiter of morality, a judge of the matter and not the manner of a work, he is no longer a critic; he is a censor.

And just what is the *content* of *The American Dream* (a comedy, yet) that so upsets these guardians of the public morality? The play is an examination of the American Scene, an attack on the substitution of artificial for real values in our society, a condemnation of complacency, cruelty, emasculation and vacuity; it is a stand against the fiction that everything in this slipping land of ours is peachy-keen.

Is the play offensive? I certainly hope so; it was my intention to offend — as well as amuse and entertain. Is it nihilist, immoral, defeatist? Well, to that let me answer that *The American Dream* is a picture of our time — as I see it, of course. Every honest work is a personal, private yowl, a statement of one individual's pleasure or pain; but I hope that *The American Dream* is something more than that. I hope that it transcends the personal and the private, and has something to do with the anguish of us all.

E. A.

New York City
  May 24th, 1961

THE AMERICAN DREAM

The Players: MOMMY
DADDY
GRANDMA
MRS BARKER
YOUNG MAN

A living-room. Two armchairs, one towards either side of the stage, facing each other diagonally out towards the audience. Against the rear wall, a sofa. A door, leading out from the apartment, in the rear wall, far stage-right. An archway, leading to other rooms, in the side wall, stage-left.

At the beginning, MOMMY and DADDY are seated in the armchairs, DADDY in the armchair stage-left, MOMMY in the other.

Curtain up. A silence. Then:

MOMMY. I don't know what can be keeping them.

DADDY. They're late, naturally.

MOMMY. Of course, they're late; it never fails.

DADDY. That's the way things are today, and there's nothing you can do about it.

MOMMY. You're quite right.

DADDY. When we took this apartment, they were quick enough to have me sign the lease; they were quick enough to take my check for two months' rent in advance ...

MOMMY. And one month's security ...

DADDY. ... and one month's security. They were quick enough to check my references; they were quick enough about all

that. But now! But now, try to get the icebox fixed, try
to get the doorbell fixed, try to get the leak in the johnny
fixed! Just try it ... they aren't so quick about *that*.

MOMMY. Of course not; it never fails. People think they can
get away with anything these days ... and, of course they
can. I went to buy a new hat yesterday.

(*Pause.*)

I said, I went to buy a new hat yesterday.

DADDY. Oh! Yes ... yes.

MOMMY. Pay attention.

DADDY. I *am* paying attention, Mommy.

MOMMY. Well, be sure you do.

DADDY. Oh, I am.

MOMMY. All right, Daddy; now listen.

DADDY. I'm listening, Mommy.

MOMMY. You're sure!

DADDY. Yes ... yes, I'm sure. I'm all ears.

MOMMY (*giggles at the thought; then —*) All right, now. I went
to buy a new hat yesterday and I said, 'I'd like a new hat,
please.' And so, they showed me a few hats, green ones and
blue ones, and I didn't like any of them, not one bit.
What did I say? What did I just say?

DADDY. You didn't like any of them, not one bit.

MOMMY. That's right; you just keep paying attention. And then
they showed me one that I did like. It was a lovely little
hat, and I said, 'Oh, this is a lovely little hat; I'll take this
hat; oh my, it's lovely. What colour is it?' And they
said, 'Why, this is beige; isn't it a lovely little beige hat?'
And I said, 'Oh, it's just lovely.' And so, I bought it.

(*Stops, looks at* DADDY.)

DADDY (*to show he is paying attention*). And so you bought it.

MOMMY. And so I bought it, and I walked out of the store with
the hat right on my head, and I ran spang into the chairman

16

of our woman's club, and she said, 'Oh, my dear, isn't that a lovely little hat? Where did you get that lovely little hat? It's the loveliest little hat; I've always wanted a wheat-coloured hat *myself*.' And I said, 'Why, no, my dear; this hat is beige; beige.' And she laughed and said, 'Why no, my dear, that's a wheat-coloured hat ... wheat. I know beige from wheat.' And I said, 'Well, my dear, I know beige from wheat, too.' What did I say? What did I just say?

DADDY (*tonelessly*). Well, my dear, I know beige from wheat, too.

MOMMY. That's right. And she laughed, and she said, 'Well, my dear, they certainly put one over on you. That's wheat if I ever saw wheat. But it's lovely, just the same.' And then she walked off. She's a dreadful woman, you don't know her; she has dreadful taste, two dreadful children, a dreadful house, and an absolutely adorable husband who sits in a wheel chair all the time. You don't know him. You don't know anybody, do you? She's just a dreadful woman, but she *is* chairman of our woman's club, so naturally I'm terribly fond of her. So, I went right back into the hat shop, and I said, 'Look here; what do you mean selling me a hat that you say is beige, when it's wheat all the time ... wheat! I can tell beige from wheat any day in the week, but not in this artificial light of yours.' They have artificial light, Daddy.

DADDY. Have they!

MOMMY. And I said, 'The minute I got outside I could tell that it wasn't a beige hat at all; it was a wheat hat.' And they said to me, 'How could you tell that when you had the hat on the top of your head?' Well, that made me angry, and so I made a scene right there; I screamed as hard as I could; I took my hat off and I threw it down on the counter, and oh, I made a terrible scene. I said, I made a terrible scene.

DADDY (*snapping to*). Yes … yes … good for you!

MOMMY. And I made an absolutely terrible scene; and they became frightened, and they said, 'Oh, madam; oh, madam.' But I kept right on, and finally they admitted that they might have made a mistake; so they took my hat into the back, and then they came out again with a hat that looked exactly like it. I took one look at it, and I said, 'This hat is wheat-coloured; wheat.' Well, of course, they said, 'Oh, no, madam, this hat is beige; you go outside and see.' So, I went outside, and lo and behold, it *was* beige. So I bought it.

DADDY (*clearing his throat*). I would imagine that it was the same hat they tried to sell you before.

MOMMY (*with a little laugh*). Well, of course it was!

DADDY. That's the way things are today; you just can't get satisfaction; you just try.

MOMMY. Well, *I* got satisfaction.

DADDY. That's right, Mommy. *You did* get satisfaction, didn't you?

MOMMY. Why are they so late? I don't know what can be keeping them.

DADDY. I've been trying for two weeks to have the leak in the johnny fixed.

MOMMY. You can't get satisfaction; just try. *I* can get satisfaction, but you can't.

DADDY. I've been trying for two weeks and it isn't so much for my sake; I can always go to the club.

MOMMY. It isn't so much for my sake, either; I can always go shopping.

DADDY. It's really for Grandma's sake.

MOMMY. Of course it's for Grandma's sake. Grandma cries

every time she goes to the johnny as it is; but now that it doesn't work it's even worse, it makes Grandma think she's getting feeble-headed.

DADDY. Grandma *is* getting feeble-headed.

MOMMY. Of course Grandma is getting feeble-headed, but not about her johnny-do's.

DADDY. No; that's true. I must have it fixed.

MOMMY. Why are they so late? I don't know what can be keeping them.

DADDY. When they came here the first time, they were ten minutes early; they were quick enough about it then.

(*Enter* GRANDMA *from the archway, stage-left. She is loaded down with boxes, large and small, neatly wrapped and tied.*)

MOMMY. Why Grandma, look at you! What *is* all that you're carrying?

GRANDMA. They're boxes. What do they look like?

MOMMY. Daddy! Look at Grandma; look at all the boxes she's carrying!

DADDY. My goodness, Grandma; look at all those boxes.

GRANDMA. Where'll I put them?

MOMMY. Heavens! I don't know. Whatever are they for?

GRANDMA. That's nobody's damn business.

MOMMY. Well, in that case, put them down next to Daddy; there.

GRANDMA (*dumping the boxes down, on and around* DADDY'*s feet*). I sure wish you'd get the john fixed.

DADDY. Oh, I do wish they'd come and fix it. We hear you ... for hours ... whimpering away....

MOMMY. Daddy! What a terrible thing to say to Grandma!

GRANDMA. Yeah. For shame, talking to me that way.

DADDY. I'm sorry, Grandma.

MOMMY. Daddy's sorry, Grandma.

GRANDMA. Well, all right. In that case I'll go get the rest of the boxes. I suppose I deserve being talked to that way. I've gotten so old. Most people think that when you get so old, you either freeze to death, or you burn up. But you don't. When you get so old, all that happens is that people talk to you that way.

DADDY (*contrite*). I said I'm sorry, Grandma.

MOMMY. Daddy said he was sorry.

GRANDMA. Well, that's all that counts. People being sorry. Makes you feel better; gives you a sense of dignity, and that's all that's important ... a sense of dignity. And it doesn't matter if you don't care, or not, either. You got to have a sense of dignity, even if you don't care, 'cause, if you don't have that, civilization's doomed.

MOMMY. You've been reading my book club selections again!

DADDY. How dare you read Mommy's book club selections, Grandma!

GRANDMA. Because I'm old! When you're old you gotta do something. When you get old, you can't talk to people because people snap at you. When you get so old, people talk to you that way. That's why you become deaf, so you won't be able to hear people talking to you that way. And that's why you go and hide under the covers in the big soft bed, so you won't feel the house shaking from people talking to you that way. That's why old people die, eventually. People talk to them that way. I've got to go and get the rest of the boxes.

(GRANDMA *exits*.)

DADDY. Poor Grandma, I didn't mean to hurt her.

MOMMY. Don't you worry about it; Grandma doesn't know what she means.

DADDY. She knows what she says, though.

MOMMY. Don't you worry about it; she won't know that soon. I love Grandma.

THE AMERICAN DREAM

DADDY. I love her, too. Look how nicely she wrapped these boxes.

MOMMY. Grandma has always wrapped boxes nicely. When I was a little girl, I was very poor, and Grandma was very poor, too, because Grandpa was in heaven. And every day, when I went to school, Grandma used to wrap a box for me, and I used to take it with me to school; and when it was lunch-time, all the little boys and girls used to take out their boxes of lunch, and they weren't wrapped nicely at all, and they used to open them and eat their chicken legs and chocolate cakes; and I used to say, 'Oh, look at my lovely lunch box; it's so nicely wrapped it would break my heart to open it.' And so, I wouldn't open it.

DADDY. Because it was empty.

MOMMY. Oh no. Grandma always filled it up, because she never ate the dinner she cooked the evening before; she gave me all her food for my lunch box the next day. After school, I'd take the box back to Grandma, and she'd open it and eat the chicken legs and chocolate cake that was inside. Grandma used to say, 'I love day-old cake.' That's where the expression day-old cake came from. Grandma always ate everything a day late. I used to eat all the other little boys' and girls' food at school, because they thought my lunch box was empty. They thought my lunch box was empty, and that's why I wouldn't open it. They thought I suffered from the sin of pride, and since that made them better than me, they were very generous.

DADDY. You were a very deceitful little girl.

MOMMY. We were very poor! But then I married you, Daddy, and now we're very rich.

DADDY. Grandma isn't rich.

MOMMY. No, but you've been so good to Grandma she feels

21

rich. She doesn't know you'd like to put her in a nursing home.

DADDY. I wouldn't!

MOMMY. Well, heaven knows, *I* would! I can't stand it, watching her do the cooking and the housework, polishing the silver, moving the furniture....

DADDY. She likes to do that. She says it's the least she can do to earn her keep.

MOMMY. Well, she's right. You can't live off people. I can live off you, because I married you. And aren't you lucky all I brought with me was Grandma. A lot of women I know would have brought their whole families to live off you. All I brought was Grandma. Grandma is all the family I have.

DADDY. I feel very fortunate.

MOMMY. You should. I have a right to live off of you because I married you, and because I used to let you get on top of me and bump your uglies; and I have a right to all your money when you die. And when you do, Grandma and I can live by ourselves ... if she's still here. Unless you have her put away in a nursing home.

DADDY. I have no intention of putting her in a nursing home.

MOMMY. Well, I wish somebody would do something with her!

DADDY. At any rate, you're very well provided for.

MOMMY. You're my sweet Daddy; that's very nice.

DADDY. I love my Mommy.

(*Enter* GRANDMA *again, laden with more boxes.*)

GRANDMA (*dumping the boxes on and around* DADDY's *feet*). There; that's the lot of them.

DADDY. They're wrapped so nicely.

GRANDMA (*to* DADDY). You won't get on my sweet side that way ...

22

MOMMY. Grandma!

GRANDMA. ... telling me how nicely I wrap boxes. Not after what you said: how I whimpered for hours....

MOMMY. Grandma!

GRANDMA (*to* MOMMY). Shut up! (*to* DADDY) You don't have any feelings, that's what's wrong with you. Old people make all sorts of noises, half of them they can't help. Old people whimper, and cry, and belch, and make great hollow rumbling sounds at the table; old people wake up in the middle of the night screaming, and find out they haven't even been asleep; and when old people *are* asleep, they try to wake up, and they can't ... not for the longest time.

MOMMY. Homilies, homilies!

GRANDMA. And there's more, too.

DADDY. I'm really very sorry, Grandma.

GRANDMA. I know you are, Daddy; it's Mommy over there makes all the trouble. If you'd listened to me, you wouldn't have married her in the first place. She was a tramp and a trollop and a trull to boot, and she's no better now.

MOMMY. Grandma!

GRANDMA (*to* MOMMY). Shut up! (*to* DADDY) When she was no more than eight years old she used to climb up on my lap and say, in a sickening little voice, 'When I gwo up, I'm going to mahwy a wich old man; I'm going to set my wittle were end right down in a tub o' butter, that's what I'm going to do.' And I warned you, Daddy; I told you to stay away from her type. I told you to. I did.

MOMMY. You stop that! You're my mother, not his!

GRANDMA. I am?

DADDY. That's right, Grandma. Mommy's right.

GRANDMA. Well, how would you expect somebody as old as I am to remember a thing like that? You don't make

23

allowances for people. I want an allowance. I want an allowance!

DADDY. All right, Grandma; I'll see to it.

MOMMY. Grandma! I'm ashamed of you.

GRANDMA. Humf! It's a fine time to say that. You should have gotten rid of me a long time ago if that's the way you feel. You should have had Daddy set me up in business somewhere ... I could have gone into the fur business, or I could have been a singer. But no; not you. You wanted me around so you could sleep in my room when Daddy got fresh. But now it isn't important, because Daddy doesn't want to get fresh with you any more, and I don't blame him. You'd rather sleep with me, wouldn't you, Daddy?

MOMMY. Daddy doesn't want to sleep with anyone. Daddy's been sick.

DADDY. I've been sick. I don't even want to sleep in the apartment.

MOMMY. You see? I told you.

DADDY. I just want to get everything over with.

MOMMY. That's right. Why are they so late? Why can't they get here on time?

GRANDMA (*an owl*). Who? Who? ... Who? Who?

MOMMY. You know, Grandma.

GRANDMA. No, I don't.

MOMMY. Well, it doesn't really matter whether you do or not.

DADDY. Is that true?

MOMMY. Oh, more or less. Look how pretty Grandma wrapped these boxes.

GRANDMA. I didn't really like wrapping them; it hurt my fingers, and it frightened me. But it had to be done.

MOMMY. Why, Grandma?

GRANDMA. None of your damn business.

24

MOMMY. Go to bed.

GRANDMA. I don't want to go to bed. I just got up. I want to stay here and watch. Besides ...

MOMMY. Go to bed.

DADDY. Let her stay up, Mommy; it isn't noon yet.

GRANDMA. I want to watch; besides ...

DADDY. Let her watch, Mommy.

MOMMY. Well all right, you can watch; but don't you dare say a word.

GRANDMA. Old people are very good at listening; old people don't like to talk; old people have colitis and lavender perfume. Now I'm going to be quiet.

DADDY. She never mentioned she wanted to be a singer.

MOMMY. Oh, I forgot to tell you, but it was ages ago.

(*The doorbell rings.*)

Oh, goodness! Here they are!

GRANDMA. Who? Who?

MOMMY. Oh, just some people.

GRANDMA. The van people? Is it the van people? Have you finally done it? Have you called the van people to come and take me away?

DADDY. Of course not, Grandma!

GRANDMA. Oh, don't be too sure. She'd have you carted off too, if she thought she could get away with it.

MOMMY. Pay no attention to her, Daddy. (*An aside to* GRANDMA.) My God, you're ungrateful!

(*The doorbell rings again.*)

DADDY (*wringing his hands.*) Oh dear; oh dear.

MOMMY (*still to* GRANDMA). Just you wait; I'll fix your wagon. (*Now to* DADDY —) Well, go let them in Daddy. What are you waiting for?

DADDY. I think we should talk about it some more. Maybe we've been hasty ... a little hasty, perhaps.

(Doorbell rings again.)

I'd like to talk about it some more.

MOMMY. There's no need. You made up your mind; you were firm; you were masculine and decisive.

DADDY. We might consider the pros and the ...

MOMMY. I won't argue with you; it has to be done; you were right. Open the door.

DADDY. But I'm not sure that ...

MOMMY. Open the door.

DADDY. Was I firm about it?

MOMMY. Oh, so firm; so firm.

DADDY. And was I decisive?

MOMMY. SO decisive! Oh, I shivered.

DADDY. And masculine? Was I really masculine?

MOMMY. Oh, Daddy, you were so masculine; I shivered and fainted.

GRANDMA. Shivered and fainted, did she? Humf!

MOMMY. You be quiet.

GRANDMA. Old people have a right to talk to themselves; it doesn't hurt the gums, and it's comforting.

(Doorbell rings again.)

DADDY. I shall now open the door.

MOMMY. WHAT a masculine Daddy! Isn't he a masculine Daddy?

GRANDMA. Don't expect me to say anything. Old people are obscene.

MOMMY. Some of your opinions aren't so bad. You know that?

DADDY *(backing off from the door)*. Maybe we can send them away.

MOMMY. Oh, look at you! You're turning into jelly; you're indecisive; you're a woman.

DADDY. All right. Watch me now; I'm going to open the door. Watch. Watch!

MOMMY. We're watching; we're watching.

GRANDMA. *I'm* not.

DADDY. Watch now; it's opening.

(*He opens the door.*)

It's open!

(MRS BARKER *steps into the room.*)

Here they are!

MOMMY. Here they are!

GRANDMA. Where?

DADDY. Come in. You're late. But, of course, we expected you to be late; we were saying that we expected you to be late.

MOMMY. Daddy, don't be rude! We were saying that you just can't get satisfaction these days, and we were talking about you, of course. Won't you come in?

MRS BARKER. Thank you. I don't mind if I do.

MOMMY. We're very glad that you're here, late as you are. You do remember us, don't you? You were here once before. I'm Mommy, and this is Daddy, and that's Grandma, doddering there in the corner.

MRS BARKER. Hello, Mommy; hello, Daddy; and hello there, Grandma.

DADDY. Now that you're here, I don't suppose you could go away and maybe come back some other time.

MRS BARKER. Oh no; we're much too efficient for that. I said, hello there, Grandma.

MOMMY. Speak to them, Grandma.

GRANDMA. I don't see them.

DADDY. For shame, Grandma; they're here.

MRS BARKER. Yes, we're here, Grandma. I'm Mrs Barker. I remember you; don't your remember me?

GRANDMA. I don't recall. Maybe you were younger, or something.

MOMMY. Grandma! What a terrible thing to say!

MRS BARKER. Oh now, don't scold her, Mommy; for all she knows she may be right.

DADDY. Uh ... Mrs Barker, is it? Won't you sit down?

MRS BARKER. I don't mind if I do.

MOMMY. Would you like a cigarette, and a drink, and would you like to cross your legs?

MRS BARKER. You forget yourself, Mommy; I'm a professional woman. But I will cross my legs.

DADDY. Yes, make yourself comfortable.

MRS BARKER. I don't mind if I do.

GRANDMA. Are they still here?

MOMMY. Be quiet, Grandma.

MRS BARKER. Oh, we're still here. My, what an unattractive apartment you have!

MOMMY. Yes, but you don't know what a trouble it is. Let me tell you ...

DADDY. I was saying to Mommy ...

MRS BARKER. Yes, I know. I was listening outside.

DADDY. About the icebox, and ... the doorbell ... and the ...

MRS BARKER. ... and the johnny. Yes, we're very efficient; we have to know everything in our work.

DADDY. Exactly what do you do?

MOMMY. Yes, what is your work?

MRS BARKER. Well, my dear, for one thing, I'm chairman of your woman's club.

MOMMY. Don't be ridiculous. I was talking to the chairman of my woman's club just yester — Why so you are. You remember, Daddy, the lady I was telling you about? The lady with the husband who sits in the *swing*? Don't you remember?

DADDY. No ... no ....

MOMMY. Of course you do. I'm so sorry, Mrs Barker. I would

have known you anywhere, except in this artificial light. And look! You have a hat just like the one I bought yesterday.

MRS BARKER (*with a little laugh*). No, not really; this hat is cream.

MOMMY. Well, my dear, that may look like a cream hat to you, but I can ...

MRS BARKER. Now, now; you seem to forget who I am.

MOMMY. Yes, I do, don't I? Are you sure you're comfortable? Won't you take off your dress?

MRS BARKER. I don't mind if I do.
   (*She removes her dress.*)

MOMMY. There. You must feel a great deal more comfortable.

MRS BARKER. Well, I certainly *look* a great deal more comfortable.

DADDY. I'm going to blush and giggle.

MOMMY. Daddy's going to blush and giggle.

MRS BARKER (*pulling the hem of her slip above her knees*). You're lucky to have such a man for a husband.

MOMMY. Oh, don't I know it!

DADDY. I just blushed and giggled and went sticky wet.

MOMMY. Isn't Daddy a caution, Mrs Barker?

MRS BARKER. Maybe if I smoked ... ?

MOMMY. Oh, that isn't necessary.

MRS BARKER. I don't mind if I do.

MOMMY. No; no, don't. Really.

MRS BARKER. I don't mind ...

MOMMY. I won't have you smoking in my house, and that's that! You're a professional woman.

DADDY. Grandma drinks AND smokes; don't you, Grandma?

GRANDMA. No.

MOMMY. Well, now, Mrs Barker; suppose you tell us why you're here.

GRANDMA (*as* MOMMY *walks through the boxes*). The boxes ... the boxes ...

MOMMY. Be quiet, Grandma.

DADDY. What did you say, Grandma?

GRANDMA (*as* MOMMY *steps on several of the boxes*). The boxes, damn it!

MRS BARKER. Boxes; she said boxes. She mentioned the boxes.

DADDY. What about the boxes, Grandma? Maybe Mrs Barker is here because of the boxes. Is that what you meant, Grandma?

GRANDMA. I don't know if that's what I meant or not. It's certainly not what I *thought* I meant.

DADDY. Grandma is of the opinion that ...

MRS BARKER. Can we assume that the boxes are for us? I mean, can we assume that you had us come here for the boxes?

MOMMY. Are you in the habit of receiving boxes?

DADDY. A very good question.

MRS BARKER. Well, that would depend on the reason we're here. I've got my fingers in so many little pies, you know. Now, I can think of one of my little activities in which we are in the habit of receiving *baskets*; but more in a literary sense than really. We *might* receive boxes, though, under very special circumstances. I'm afraid that's the best answer I can give you.

DADDY. It's a very interesting answer.

MRS BARKER. *I* thought so. But, does it help?

MOMMY. No; I'm afraid not.

DADDY. I wonder if it might help us any if I said I feel misgivings, that I have definite qualms.

MOMMY. Where, Daddy?

DADDY. Well, mostly right here, right around where the stitches were.

MOMMY. Daddy had an operation, you know.

MRS BARKER. Oh, you poor Daddy! I didn't know; but then, how could I?

GRANDMA. You might have asked; it wouldn't have hurt you.

MOMMY. Dry up, Grandma.

GRANDMA. There you go. Letting your true feelings come out. Old people aren't dry enough, I suppose. My sacks are empty, the fluid in my eyeballs is all caked on the inside edges, my spine is made of sugar candy, I breathe ice; but you don't hear me complain. Nobody hears old people complain because people think that's all old people do. And *that's* because old people are gnarled and sagged and twisted into the shape of a complaint.

(*Signs off.*)

That's all.

MRS BARKER. What was wrong, Daddy?

DADDY. Well, you know how it is: the doctors took out something that was there and put in something that wasn't there. An operation.

MRS BARKER. You're very fortunate, I should say.

MOMMY. Oh, he is; he is. All his life, Daddy has wanted to be a United States Senator; but now ... why now he's changed his mind, and for the rest of his life he's going to want to be Governor ... it would be nearer the apartment, you know.

MRS BARKER. You *are* fortunate, Daddy.

DADDY. Yes, indeed; except that I get these qualms now and then, definite ones.

MRS BARKER. Well, it's just a matter of things settling; you're like an old house.

MOMMY. Why Daddy, thank Mrs Barker.

DADDY. Thank you.

MRS BARKER. Ambition! That's the ticket. I have a brother who's very much like you, Daddy ... ambitious. Of course, he's a great deal younger than you; he's even younger than I am ... if such a thing is possible. He runs a little newspaper. Just a little newspaper ... but he runs it. He's chief cook and bottle washer of that little newspaper, which he calls *The Village Idiot*. He has such a sense of humour; he's so self-deprecating, so modest. And he'd never admit it himself, but he *is* the Village Idiot.

MOMMY. Oh, I think that's just grand. Don't you think so, Daddy?

DADDY. Yes, just grand.

MRS BARKER. My brother's a dear man, and he has a dear little wife, whom he loves, dearly. He loves her so much he just can't get a sentence out without mentioning her. He wants everybody to know he's married. He's really a stickler on that point; he can't be introduced to anybody and say hello without adding, 'Of course, I'm married.' As far as I'm concerned, he's the chief exponent of Woman Love in this whole country; he's even been written up in psychiatric journals because of it.

DADDY. Indeed!

MOMMY. Isn't that lovely.

MRS BARKER. Oh, I think so. There's too much woman hatred in this country, and that's a fact.

GRANDMA. Oh, I don't know.

MOMMY. Oh, I think that's just grand. Don't you think so, Daddy?

DADDY. Yes, just grand.

GRANDMA. In case anybody's interested ...

MOMMY. Be quiet, Grandma.

GRANDMA. Nuts!

MOMMY. Oh, Mrs Barker, you *must* forgive Grandma. She's rural.

MRS BARKER. I don't mind if I do.

DADDY. Maybe Grandma has something to say.

MOMMY. Nonsense. Old people have nothing to say; and if old people *did* have something to say, nobody would listen to them. (*to* GRANDMA) You see! I can pull that stuff just as easy as you can.

GRANDMA. Well, you got the rhythm, but you don't really have the quality. Besides, you're middle-aged.

MOMMY. I'm proud of it!

GRANDMA. Look. I'll show you how it's really done. Middle-aged people think they can do anything, but the truth is that middle-aged people can't do most things as well as they used to. Middle-aged people think they're special because they're like everybody else. We live in the age of deformity. You see? Rhythm *and* content. You'll learn.

DADDY. I do wish I weren't surrounded by women; I'd like some men around here.

MRS BARKER. You can say that again!

GRANDMA. I don't hardly count as a woman, so can I say my piece?

MOMMY. Go on. Jabber away.

GRANDMA. It's very simple; the fact is, these boxes don't have anything to do with why this good lady is come to call. Now, if you're interested in knowing why these boxes *are* here ...

DADDY. I'm sure that must be all very true, Grandma, but what does it have to do with why ... pardon me, what is that name again?

MRS BARKER. Mrs Barker.

DADDY. Exactly. What does it have to do with why ... that name again?

MRS BARKER. Mrs Barker.

DADDY. Precisely. What does it have to do with why what's-her-name is here?

MOMMY. They're here because we asked them.

MRS BARKER. Yes. That's why.

GRANDMA. Now if you're interested in knowing why these boxes *are* here ...

MOMMY. Well, nobody *is* interested!

GRANDMA. You can be as snippety as you like for all the good it'll do you.

DADDY. You two will have to stop arguing.

MOMMY. I don't argue with her.

DADDY. No, now, perhaps I can go away myself....

MOMMY. Well, one or the other; the way things are now it's impossible. In the first place, it's too crowded in this apartment. (*to* GRANDMA) And it's you that takes up all the space, with your enema bottles, and your Pekinese, and God-only-knows-what-else ... and now all these boxes....

GRANDMA. These boxes are ...

MRS BARKER. I've never heard of enema *bottles*....

GRANDMA. She means enema bags, but she doesn't know the difference. Mommy comes from extremely bad stock. And besides, when Mommy was born ... well, it was a difficult delivery, and she had a head shaped like a banana.

MOMMY. You ungrateful — Daddy? Daddy, you see how ungrateful she is after all these years, after all the things we've done for her? (*to* GRANDMA) One of these days you're going away in a van; that's what's going to happen to you!

GRANDMA. Do tell!

MRS BARKER. Like a banana?

GRANDMA. Yup, just like a banana.

MRS BARKER. My word!

MOMMY. You stop listening to her; she'll say anything. Just the other night she called Daddy a hedgehog.

34

MRS BARKER. She didn't!

GRANDMA. That's right, baby; you stick up for me.

MOMMY. I don't know where she gets the words; on the television, maybe.

MRS BARKER. Did you really call him a hedgehog?

GRANDMA. Oh look; what difference does it make whether I did or not?

DADDY. Grandma's right. Leave Grandma alone.

MOMMY (to DADDY). How dare you!

GRANDMA. Oh, leave her alone, Daddy; the kid's all mixed up.

MOMMY. You see? I told you. It's all those television shows. Daddy, you go right into Grandma's room and take her television and shake all the tubes loose.

DADDY. Don't mention tubes to me.

MOMMY. Oh! Mommy forgot! (to MRS BARKER) Daddy has tubes now, where he used to have tracts.

MRS BARKER. Is that a fact!

GRANDMA. I know why this dear lady is here.

MOMMY. You be still.

MRS BARKER. Oh, I do wish you'd tell me.

MOMMY. No! No! That wouldn't be fair at all.

DADDY. Besides, she knows why she's here; she's here because we called them.

MRS BARKER. La! But that still leaves me puzzled. I know I'm here because you called us, but I'm such a busy girl, with this committee and that committee, and the Responsible Citizens Activities I indulge in.

MOMMY. Oh my; busy, busy.

MRS BARKER. Yes, indeed. So I'm afraid you'll have to give me some help.

MOMMY. Oh, no. No, you must be mistaken. I can't believe we asked you here to give you any help. With the way taxes

are these days, and the way you can't get satisfaction in
ANYTHING ... no, I don't believe so.

DADDY. And if you need help ... why, I should think you'd
apply for a Fulbright Scholarship....

MOMMY. And if not that ... why, then a Guggenheim Fellow-
ship....

GRANDMA. Oh, come on; why not shoot the works and try for
the Prix de Rome. (*under her breath to* MOMMY *and* DADDY)
Beasts!

MRS BARKER. Oh, what a jolly family. But let me think. I'm
knee-deep in work these days; there's the Ladies' Auxiliary
Air Raid Committee, for one thing; how do you feel about
air raids?

MOMMY. Oh, I'd say we're hostile.

DADDY. Yes, definitely; we're hostile.

MRS BARKER. Then, you'll be no help there. There's too much
hostility in the world these days as it is; but I'll not
badger you! There's a surfeit of badgers as well.

GRANDMA. While we're at it, there's been a run on old people,
too. The Department of Agriculture, or maybe it wasn't
the Department of Agriculture — anyway, it was some
department that's run by a girl — put out figures showing
that ninety per cent of the adult population of the country
is over eighty years old ... or eighty per cent is over
ninety years old ...

MOMMY. You're such a liar! You just finished saying that
everyone is middle-aged.

GRANDMA. I'm just telling you what the government says ...
that doesn't have anything to do with what ...

MOMMY. It's that television! Daddy, go break her television.

GRANDMA. You won't find it.

DADDY (*wearily getting up*). If I must ... I must.

MOMMY. And don't step on the Pekinese; it's blind.

36

DADDY. It may be blind, but Daddy isn't.

(*He exits, through the archway, stage-left.*)

GRANDMA. You won't find *it*, either.

MOMMY. Oh, I'm so fortunate to have such a husband. Just think: I could have a husband who was poor, or argumentative, or a husband who sat in a wheel chair all day … OOOOHHHH! *What* have I said? What *have* I said?

GRANDMA. You said you could have a husband who sat in a wheel …

MOMMY. I'm mortified! I could die! I could cut my tongue out! I could …

MRS BARKER (*forcing a smile*). Oh, now … now … don't think about it …

MOMMY. I could … why, I could …

MRS BARKER. … don't think about it … really.…

MOMMY. You're quite right. I won't think about it, and that way I'll forget that I ever said it, and that way it will be all right.

(*Pause.*)

There … I've forgotten. Well, now, now that Daddy is out of the room we can have some girl talk.

MRS BARKER. I'm not sure that I …

MOMMY. You *do* want to have some girl talk, don't you?

MRS BARKER. I was going to say I'm not sure that I wouldn't care for a glass of water. I feel a little faint.

MOMMY. Grandma, go get Mrs Barker a glass of water.

GRANDMA. Go get it yourself. I quit.

MOMMY. Grandma loves to do little things around the house; it gives her a false sense of security.

GRANDMA. I quit! I'm through!

MOMMY. Now, you be a good Grandma, or you know what will happen to you. You'll be taken away in a van.

GRANDMA. You don't frighten me. I'm too old to be frightened. Besides ...

MOMMY. WELL! I'll tend to you later. I'll hide your teeth ... I'll ...

GRANDMA. Everything's hidden.

MRS BARKER. I *am* going to faint. I *am*.

MOMMY. Good heavens! I'll go myself.

(*As she exits, through the archway, stage-left —*)

I'll fix you, Grandma. I'll take care of you later.

(*She exits.*)

GRANDMA. Oh, go soak your head. (*to* MRS BARKER) Well, dearie, how do you feel?

MRS BARKER. A little better, I think. Yes, much better, thank you, Grandma.

GRANDMA. That's good.

MRS BARKER. But ... I feel so lost ... not knowing why I'm here ... and, on top of it, they say I was here before.

GRANDMA. Well, you were. You weren't *here*, exactly, because we've moved around a lot, from one apartment to another, up and down the social ladder like mice, if you like similes.

MRS BARKER. I don't ... particularly.

GRANDMA. Well, then, I'm sorry.

MRS BARKER (*suddenly*). Grandma, I feel I can trust you.

GRANDMA. Don't be too sure; it's every man for himself around this place....

MRS BARKER. Oh ... is it? None the less, I really do feel that I can trust you. *Please* tell me why they called and asked us to come. I implore you!

GRANDMA. Oh my; that feels good. It's been so long since anybody implored me. Do it again. Implore me some more.

MRS BARKER. You're your daughter's mother, all right!

GRANDMA. Oh, I don't mean to be hard. If you won't implore

38

me, then beg me, or ask me, or entreat me ... just anything like that.

MRS BARKER. You're a dreadful old woman!

GRANDMA. You'll understand some day. Please!

MRS BARKER. Oh, for heaven's sake! ... I implore you ... I beg you ... I beseech you!

GRANDMA. Beseech! Oh, that's the nicest word I've heard in ages. You're a dear, sweet woman.... You ... beseech ... me. I can't resist that.

MRS BARKER. Well, then ... please tell me why they asked us to come.

GRANDMA. Well, I'll give you a hint. That's the best I can do, because I'm a muddleheaded old woman. Now listen, because it's important. Once upon a time, not too very long ago, but a long enough time ago ... oh, about twenty years ago ... there was a man very much like Daddy, and a woman very much like Mommy, who were married to each other, very much like Mommy and Daddy are married to each other; and they lived in an apartment very much like one that's very much like this one, and they lived there with an old woman who was very much like yours truly, only younger, because it was some time ago; in fact, they were all somewhat younger.

MRS BARKER. How fascinating!

GRANDMA. Now, at the same time, there was a dear lady very much like you, only younger then, who did all sorts of Good Works.... And one of the Good Works this dear lady did was in something very much like a volunteer capacity for an organization very much like the Bye-Bye Adoption Service, which is near by and which was run by a terribly deaf old lady very much like the Miss Bye-Bye who runs the Bye-Bye Adoption Service near by.

MRS BARKER. How enthralling!

39

GRANDMA. Well, be that as it may. None the less, one afternoon this man, who was very much like Daddy, and this woman who was very much like Mommy came to see this dear lady who did all the Good Works, who was very much like you, dear, and they were very sad and very hopeful, and they cried and smiled and bit their fingers, and they said all the most intimate things.

MRS BARKER. How spellbinding! What did they say?

GRANDMA. Well, it was very sweet. The woman, who was very much like Mommy, said that she and the man who was very much like Daddy had never been blessed with anything very much like a bumble of joy.

MRS BARKER. A what?

GRANDMA. A bumble; a bumble of joy.

MRS BARKER. Oh, like bundle.

GRANDMA. Well, yes; very much like it. Bundle, bumble; who cares? At any rate, the woman, who was very much like Mommy, said that they wanted a bumble of their own, but that the man, who was very much like Daddy, couldn't have a bumble; and the man, who was very much like Daddy, said that yes, they had wanted a bumble of their own, but that the woman, who was very much like Mommy, couldn't have one, and that now they wanted to buy something very much like a bumble.

MRS BARKER. How engrossing!

GRANDMA. Yes. And the dear lady, who was very much like you, said something that was very much like, 'Oh, what a shame; but take heart ... I think we have just the bumble *for* you.' And, well, the lady, who was very much like Mommy, and the man, who was very much like Daddy, cried and smiled and bit their fingers, and said some more intimate things, which were totally irrelevant but which were pretty hot stuff, and so the dear lady, who was very much like you, and who had something very much like a penchant for pornography, listened with something very much like enthusiasm. 'Whee,' she said. 'Whooopeeeeee!' But that's beside the point.

MRS BARKER. I suppose *so*. But how gripping!

GRANDMA. Anyway ... they *bought* something very much like a bumble, and they took it away with them. But ... things didn't work out very well.

MRS BARKER. You mean there was trouble?

GRANDMA You got it. (*with a glance through the archway*) But, I'm going to have to speed up now because I think I'm leaving soon.

MRS BARKER. Oh. Are you really?

GRANDMA. Yup.

MRS BARKER. But old people don't go anywhere; they're either taken places, or put places.

GRANDMA. Well, this old person is different. Anyway ... things started going badly.

MRS BARKER. Oh yes. Yes.

GRANDMA. Weeeeellll ... in the first place, it turned out the bumble didn't look like either one of its parents. That was enough of a blow, but things got worse. One night, it cried its heart out, if you can imagine such a thing.

MRS BARKER. Cried its heart out! Well!

GRANDMA. But that was only the beginning. Then it turned out it only had eyes for its Daddy.

MRS BARKER. For its Daddy! Why, any self-respecting woman would have gouged those eyes right out of its head.

GRANDMA. Well, she did. That's exactly what she did. But then, it kept its nose up in the air.

MRS BARKER. Ufggh! How disgusting!

GRANDMA. That's what they thought. But *then*, it began to develop an interest in its you-know-what.

MRS BARKER. In its you-know-what! Well! I hope they cut its hands off at the wrists!

GRANDMA. Well, yes, they did that eventually. But first, they cut off its you-know-what.

MRS BARKER. A much better idea!

GRANDMA. That's what they thought. But after they cut off its you-know-what, it *still* put its hands under the covers, *looking* for its you-know-what. So, finally, they *had* to cut off its hands at the wrists.

MRS BARKER. Naturally!

GRANDMA. And it was such a resentful bumble. Why, one day it called its Mommy a dirty name.

MRS BARKER. Well, I hope they cut its tongue out!

GRANDMA. Of course. And then, as it got bigger, they found out all sorts of terrible things about it, like: it didn't have a head on its shoulders, it had no guts, it was spineless, its feet were made of clay ... just dreadful things.

MRS BARKER. Dreadful!

GRANDMA. So you can understand how they became discouraged.

MRS BARKER. I certainly can! And what did they do?

GRANDMA. What did they do? Well for the last straw, it finally up and died; and you can imagine how *that* made them feel, their having paid for it, and all. So, they called up the lady who sold them the bumble in the first place and told her to come right over to their apartment. They wanted satisfaction; they wanted their money back. That's what they wanted.

MRS BARKER. My, my, my.

GRANDMA. How do you like *them* apples?

MRS BARKER. My, my, my.

DADDY (*off stage*). Mommy! I can't find Grandma's television, and I can't find the Pekinese, either.

MOMMY (*off stage*). Isn't that funny! And I can't find the water.

GRANDMA. Heh, heh, heh. I told them everything was hidden.

MRS BARKER. Did you hide the water, too?

GRANDMA (*puzzled*). No. No, I didn't do *that*.

DADDY (*off stage*). The truth of the matter is, I can't even find Grandma's room.

GRANDMA. Heh, heh, heh.

MRS BARKER. My! You certainly did hide things, didn't you?

GRANDMA. Sure, kid, sure.

MOMMY (*sticking her head in the room*). Did you ever hear of such a thing, Grandma? Daddy can't find your television, and he can't find the Pekinese, and the truth of the matter is he can't even find your room.

GRANDMA. I told you. I hid everthing.

MOMMY. Nonsense, Grandma! Just wait until I get my hands on you. You're a troublemaker ... that's what you are.

GRANDMA. Well, I'll be out of here pretty soon, baby.

MOMMY. Oh, you don't know how right you are! Daddy's been wanting to send you away for a long time now, but I've been restraining him. I'll tell you one thing, though ... I'm getting sick and tired of this fighting, and I might just let him have his way. Then you'll see what'll happen. Away you'll go; in a van, too. I'll let Daddy call the van man.

GRANDMA. I'm way ahead of you.

MOMMY. How can you be so old and so smug at the same time? You have no sense of proportion.

GRANDMA. You just answered your own question.

MOMMY. Mrs Barker, I'd much rather you came into the kitchen for that glass of water, what with Grandma out here, and all.

MRS BARKER. I don't see what Grandma has to do with it; and besides, I don't think you're very polite.

MOMMY. You seem to forget that you're a guest in this house ...

GRANDMA. Apartment!

MOMMY. Apartment! And that you're a professional woman. So, if you'll be so good as to come into the kitchen, I'll be more than happy to show you where the water is, and where the glass is, and then you can put two and two together, if you're clever enough.

(*She vanishes.*)

MRS BARKER (*after a moment's consideration*). I suppose she's right.

GRANDMA. Well, that's how it is when people call you up and ask you over to do something for them.

MRS BARKER. I suppose you're right, too. Well, Grandma, it's been very nice talking to you.

GRANDMA. And I've enjoyed listening. Say, don't tell Mommy or Daddy that I gave you that hint, will you?

MRS BARKER. Oh, dear me, the hint! I'd forgotten about it, if you can imagine such a thing. No, I won't breathe a word of it to them.

GRANDMA. I don't know if it helped you any ...

MRS BARKER. I can't tell, yet. I'll have to ... what *is* the word I want? ... I'll have to relate it ... that's it ... I'll have to relate it to certain things that I *know*, and ... draw ... conclusions.... What I'll really have to do is to see if it applies to anything. I mean, after all, I *do* do volunteer work for an adoption service, but it isn't very much *like* the Bye-Bye Adoption Service ... it *is* the Bye-Bye Adoption Service ... and while I can remember Mommy and Daddy coming to see me, oh, about twenty years ago, about buying a bumble, I can't quite remember anyone very much *like* Mommy and Daddy coming to see me

44

about buying a bumble. Don't you see? It really presents quite a problem .... I'll have to think about it ... mull it ... but at any rate, it was truly first-class of you to try to help me. Oh, will you still be here after I've had my drink of water?

GRANDMA. Probably ... I'm not as spry as I used to be.

MRS BARKER. Oh. Well, I won't say goodbye then.

GRANDMA. No. Don't.

(MRS BARKER *exits through the archway.*)

People don't say goodbye to old people because they think they'll frighten them. Lordy! If they only knew how awful 'hello' and 'my, you're looking chipper' sounded, they wouldn't say those things either. The truth is, there isn't much you *can* say to old people that doesn't sound just terrible.

(*The doorbell rings.*)

Come on in!

(*The* YOUNG MAN *enters.* GRANDMA *looks him over.*)

Well, now, aren't you a breath of fresh air!

YOUNG MAN. Hello there.

GRANDMA. My, my, my. Are you the van man?

YOUNG MAN. The what?

GRANDMA. The van man. The van man. Are you come to take me away?

YOUNG MAN. I don't know what you're talking about.

GRANDMA. Oh.

(*Pause.*)

Well.

(*Pause.*)

My, my, aren't you something!

YOUNG MAN. Hm?

GRANDMA. I said, my, my, aren't you something.

YOUNG MAN. Oh. Thank you.

45

GRANDMA. You don't sound very enthusiastic.

YOUNG MAN. Oh, I'm ... I'm used to it.

GRANDMA. Yup ... yup. You know, if I were about a hundred and fifty years younger I could go for you.

YOUNG MAN. Yes, I imagine so.

GRANDMA. Unh-hunh ... will you look at those muscles!

YOUNG MAN (*flexing his muscles*). Yes, they're quite good, aren't they?

GRANDMA. Boy, they sure are. They natural?

YOUNG MAN. Well the basic structure was there, but I've done some work, too ... you know, in a gym.

GRANDMA. I'll bet you have. You ought to be in the movies, boy.

YOUNG MAN. I know.

GRANDMA. Yup! Right up there on the old silver screen. But I suppose you've heard that before.

YOUNG MAN. Yes, I have.

GRANDMA. You ought to try out for them ... the movies.

YOUNG MAN. Well, actually, I may have a career there yet. I've lived out on the West Coast almost all my life ... and I've met a few people who ... might be able to help me. I'm not in too much of a hurry, though. I'm almost as young as I look.

GRANDMA. Oh, that's nice. And will you look at that face!

YOUNG MAN. Yes, it's quite good, isn't it? Clean-cut, midwest farm boy type, almost insultingly good-looking in a typically American way. Good profile, straight nose, honest eyes, wonderful smile ...

GRANDMA. Yup. Boy, you know what you are, don't you? You're the American Dream, that's what you are. All those other people, they don't know what they're talking about. You ... *you* are the American Dream.

YOUNG MAN. Thanks.

MOMMY (*off stage*). Who rang the doorbell?

GRANDMA (*shouting off-stage*). The American Dream!

MOMMY (*off stage*). What? What was that, Grandma?

GRANDMA (*shouting*). The American Dream! The American Dream! Damn it!

DADDY (*off stage*). How's that, Mommy?

MOMMY (*off stage*). Oh, some gibberish; pay no attention. Did you find Grandma's room?

DADDY (*off stage*). No. I can't even find Mrs Barker.

YOUNG MAN. What was all that?

GRANDMA. Oh, that was just the folks, but let's not talk about them, honey; let's talk about you.

YOUNG MAN. All right.

GRANDMA. Well, let's see. If you're not the van man, what are you doing here?

YOUNG MAN. I'm looking for work.

GRANDMA. Are you! Well, what kind of work?

YOUNG MAN. Oh, almost anything ... almost anything that pays. I'll do almost anything for money.

GRANDMA. Will you ... will you? Hmmmm. I wonder if there's anything you could do around here?

YOUNG MAN. There might be. It looked to be a likely building.

GRANDMA. It's always looked to be a rather unlikely building to me, but I suppose you'd know better than I.

YOUNG MAN. I can sense these things.

GRANDMA. There *might* be something you could do around here. Stay there! Don't come any closer.

YOUNG MAN. Sorry.

GRANDMA. I don't mean I'd *mind*. I don't know whether I'd mind, or not .... But it wouldn't look well; it would look just *awful*.

YOUNG MAN. Yes; I suppose so.

GRANDMA. Now, stay there, let me concentrate. What could

you do? The folks have been in something of a quandary around here today, sort of a dilemma, and I wonder if you mightn't be some help.

YOUNG MAN. I hope so ... if there's money in it. Do you have any money?

GRANDMA. Money! Oh, there's more money around here than you'd know what to do with.

YOUNG MAN. I'm not so sure.

GRANDMA. Well, maybe not. Besides, I've got money of my own.

YOUNG MAN. You have?

GRANDMA. Sure. Old people quite often have lots of money; more often than most people expect. Come here, so I can whisper to you ... not too close. I might faint.

YOUNG MAN. Oh, I'm sorry.

GRANDMA. It's all right, dear. Anyway ... have you ever heard of that big baking contest they run? The one where all the ladies get together in a big barn and bake away?

YOUNG MAN. I'm ... not ... sure....

GRANDMA. Not so close. Well, it doesn't matter whether you've heard of it or not. The important thing is — and I don't want anybody to hear this ... the folks think I haven't been out of the house in eight years — the important thing is that I won first prize in that baking contest this year. Oh, it was in all the papers; not under my own name, though. I used a *nom de boulangère*; I called myself Uncle Henry.

YOUNG MAN. Did you?

GRANDMA. Why not? I didn't see any reason not to. I look just as much like an old man as I do like an old woman. And you know what I called it ... what I won for?

YOUNG MAN. No. What did you call it?

GRANDMA. I called it Uncle Henry's Day-Old Cake.

YOUNG MAN. That's a very nice name.

GRANDMA. And it wasn't any trouble, either. All I did was go out and get a store-bought cake, and keep it around for a while, and then slip it in, unbeknownst to anybody. Simple.

YOUNG MAN. You're a very resourceful person.

GRANDMA. Pioneer stock.

YOUNG MAN. Is all this true? Do you want me to believe all this?

GRANDMA. Well, you can believe it or not ... it doesn't make any difference to me. All *I* know is, Uncle Henry's Day-Old Cake won me twenty-five thousand smackerolas.

YOUNG MAN. Twenty-five thou —

GRANDMA. Right on the old loggerhead. Now ... how do you like them apples?

YOUNG MAN. Love 'em.

GRANDMA. I thought you'd be impressed.

YOUNG MAN. Money talks.

GRANDMA. Hey! You look familiar.

YOUNG MAN. Hm? Pardon?

GRANDMA. I said, you look familiar.

YOUNG MAN. Well, I've done some modelling.

GRANDMA. No ... no. I don't mean that. You look familiar.

YOUNG MAN. Well, I'm a type.

GRANDMA. Yup; you sure are. Why do you say you'd do anything for money ... if you don't mind my being nosy?

YOUNG MAN. No, no. It's part of the interview. I'll be happy to tell you. It's that I have no talents at all, except what you see ... my person; my body, my face. In every other way I am incomplete, and I must therefore ... compensate.

GRANDMA. What do you mean, incomplete? You look pretty complete to me.

YOUNG MAN. I think I can explain it to you, partially because you're very old, and very old people have perceptions they keep to themselves, because if they expose them to other people ... well, you know what ridicule and neglect are.

GRANDMA. I do, child, I do.

YOUNG MAN. Then listen. My mother died the night that I was born, and I never knew my father; I doubt my mother did. But, I wasn't alone, because lying with me ... in the placenta ... there was someone else ... my brother ... my twin.

GRANDMA. Oh, my child.

YOUNG MAN. We were identical twins ... he and I ... not fraternal ... identical; we were derived from the same ovum; and in *this*, in that we were twins not from separate ova but from the same one, we had a kinship such as you cannot imagine. We ... we felt each other breathe ... his heartbeats thundered in my temples ... mine in his ... our stomachs ached and we cried for feeding at the same time ... are you old enough to understand?

GRANDMA. I think so, child; I think I'm nearly old enough.

YOUNG MAN. I hope so. But we were separated when we were still very young, my brother, my twin and I ... inasmuch as you can separate one being. We were torn apart ... thrown to opposite ends of the continent. I don't know what became of my brother ... to the rest of myself ... except that, from time to time, in the years that have passed, I have suffered losses ... that I can't explain. A fall from grace ... a departure of innocence ... loss ... loss. How can I put it to you? All right; like this: Once ... it was as if all at once my heart ... became numb ... almost as though I ... almost as though ... just like that ... it had been wrenched from my body ... and from that time I have been unable to love. Once ... I was asleep at the time ... I awoke, and my eyes were burning. And since that time I have been unable to see anything, *anything*, with pity, with affection ... with anything but ... cool disinterest. And my groin ... even there ... since one time ... one specific agony ... since then I have not been able to *love* anyone with my body. And even my hands ... I cannot touch another person and feel love. And there is more ... there are more losses, but it all comes down to this: I no longer have the capacity to feel anything. I have no emotions. I have been drained, torn asunder ... disembowelled. I have, now, only my person ... my body, my face. I use what I have ... I let people love me ... I accept the syntax around me, for while I know I cannot relate ... I know I must be related *to*. I let people love me... I let people touch me ... I let them draw pleasure from my groin ... from my presence ... from the fact of me ... but, that is all it comes to. As I told you, I am incomplete ... I can feel nothing. I can feel nothing. And so ... here I am ... as you see me. I am ... but this ... what you see. And it will always be thus.

GRANDMA. Oh, my child; my child.

(*Long pause; then —*)

I was mistaken ... before. I don't know you from somewhere, but I knew ... once ... someone very much like you ... or, very much as perhaps you were.

YOUNG MAN. Be careful; be very careful. What I have told you may not be true. In my profession ...

GRANDMA. Shhhhhh.

(*The* YOUNG MAN *bows his head, in acquiescence.*)

Someone ... to be more precise ... who might have turned out to be very much like you might have turned out to be. And ... unless I'm terribly mistaken ... you've found yourself a job.

YOUNG MAN. What are my duties?

MRS BARKER (*off stage*). Yoo-hoo! Yoo-hoo!

GRANDMA. Oh-oh. You'll ... you'll have to play it by ear, my dear ... unless I get a chance to talk to you again. I've got to go into my act, now.

YOUNG MAN. But, I ...

GRANDMA. Yoo-hoo!

MRS BARKER (*coming through archway*). Yoo-hoo.... Oh, there you are, Grandma. I'm glad to see somebody. I can't find Mommy or Daddy.

(*Double takes.*)

Well ... who's this?

GRANDMA. This? Well ... un ... oh, this is the ... uh ... the van man. That's who it is ... the van man.

MRS BARKER. So! It's true! They *did* call the van man. They *are* having you carted away.

GRANDMA (*shrugging*). Well, you know. It figures.

MRS BARKER (*to* YOUNG MAN). How dare you cart this poor old woman away!

YOUNG MAN (*after a quick look at* GRANDMA, *who nods*). I do what I'm paid to do. I don't ask any questions.

MRS BARKER (*after a brief pause*). Oh. (*Pause.*) Well, you're quite right, of course, and I shouldn't meddle.

GRANDMA (*to* YOUNG MAN). Dear, will you take my things out to the van?

(*She points to the boxes.*)

YOUNG MAN (*after only the briefest hesitation*). Why certainly.

GRANDMA (*as the* YOUNG MAN *takes up half the boxes, exits by the front door*). Isn't that a nice young van man?

MRS BARKER (*shaking her head in disbelief, watching the* YOUNG MAN *exit*). Unh-hunh ... some things have changed for the

better. I remember when I had *my* mother carted off ...
the van man who came for her wasn't anything near as
nice as this one.

GRANDMA. Oh, did you have your mother carted off, too?

MRS BARKER (*cheerfully*). Why certainly! Didn't you?

GRANDMA (*puzzling*). No ... no, I didn't. At least, I can't
remember. Listen, dear; I got to talk to you for a
second.

MRS BARKER. Why certainly, Grandma.

GRANDMA. Now, listen.

MRS BARKER. Yes, Grandma. Yes.

GRANDMA. Now listen carefully. You got this dilemma here
with Mommy and Daddy ...

MRS BARKER. Yes! I wonder where they've gone to.

GRANDMA. They'll be back in. Now, LISTEN!

MRS BARKER. Oh, I'm sorry.

GRANDMA. Now, you got this dilemma here with Mommy and
Daddy, and I think I got the way out for you.
(*The* YOUNG MAN *re-enters through the front door.*)
Will you take the rest of my things out now, dear?
(*to* MRS BARKER, *while the* YOUNG MAN *takes the rest of
the boxes, exits again by the front door.*)
Fine. Now listen, dear.
(*She begins to whisper in* MRS BARKER's *ear.*)

MRS BARKER. Oh! Oh! Oh! I don't think I could ... do you
really think I could? Well, why not? What a wonderful
idea ... what an absolutely wonderful idea!

GRANDMA. Well, yes, I thought it was.

MRS BARKER. And you so old!

GRANDMA. Heh, heh, heh.

MRS BARKER. Well, I think it's absolutely marvellous,
anyway. I'm going to find Mommy and Daddy right
now.

GRANDMA. Good. You do that.

MRS BARKER. Well, now. I think I will say goodbye. I can't thank you enough.

 (*She starts to exit through the archway.*)

GRANDMA. You're welcome. Say it!

MRS BARKER. Huh? What?

GRANDMA. Say goodbye.

MRS BARKER. Oh. Goodbye.

 (*She exits.*)

Mommy! I say, Mommy! Daddy!

GRANDMA. Goodbye.

 (*By herself now, she looks about.*)

Ah me.

 (*Shakes her head.*)

Ah me.

 (*Takes in the room.*)

Goodbye.

 (*The* YOUNG MAN *re-enters.*)

Oh, hello, there.

YOUNG MAN. All the boxes are outside.

GRANDMA (*a little sadly*). I don't know why I bother to take them with me. They don't have much in them ... some old letters, a couple of regrets ... Pekinese ... blind at that ... the television ... my Sunday teeth ... eighty-six years of living ... some sounds ... a few images, a little garbled by now ... and, well ... (*She shrugs.*) ... you know ... the things one accumulates.

YOUNG MAN. Can I get you ... a cab, or something?

GRANDMA. Oh no, dear ... thank you just the same. I'll take it from here.

YOUNG MAN. And what shall I do now?

GRANDMA. Oh, you stay here, dear. It will all become clear to you. It will be explained. You'll understand.

YOUNG MAN. Very well.

GRANDMA (*after one more look about*). Well ...

YOUNG MAN. Let me see you to the elevator.

GRANDMA. Oh ... that *would* be nice, dear.

> (*They both exit by the front door, slowly.*
> *Enter* MRS BARKER, *followed by* MOMMY *and* DADDY.)

MRS BARKER. ... and I'm happy to tell you that the whole thing's settled. Just like that.

MOMMY. Oh, we're so glad. We were afraid there might be a problem, what with delays, and all.

DADDY. Yes, we're very relieved.

MRS BARKER. Well, now; that's what professional women are for.

MOMMY. Why ... where's Grandma? Grandma's not here! Where's Grandma? And look! The boxes are gone, too. Grandma's gone, and so are the boxes. She's taken off, and she's stolen something! Daddy!

MRS BARKER. Why, Mommy, the van man was here.

MOMMY (*startled*). The what?

MRS BARKER. The van man. The van man was here.

> (*The lights might dim a little, suddenly.*)

MOMMY (*shakes her head*). No, that's impossible.

MRS BARKER. Why, I saw him with my own two eyes.

MOMMY (*near tears*). No, no, that's impossible. No. There's no such thing as the van man. There is no van man. We ... we made him up. Grandma? Grandma?

DADDY (*moving to* MOMMY). There, there, now.

MOMMY. Oh Daddy ... where's Grandma?

DADDY. There, there, now.

> (*While* DADDY *is comforting* MOMMY, GRANDMA *comes out, stage-right, near the footlights.*)

GRANDMA (*to the audience*). Shhhhhh! I want to watch this.

> (*She motions to* MRS BARKER *who, with a secret smile,*

tiptoes to the front door and opens it. The YOUNG MAN *is framed therein. Lights up full again as he steps into the room.)*

MRS BARKER. Surprise! Surprise! Here we are!

MOMMY. What? What?

DADDY. Hm? What?

MOMMY (*her tears merely sniffles now*). What surprise?

MRS BARKER. Why, I told you. The surprise I told you about.

DADDY. You ... you know, Mommy.

MOMMY. Sur ... prise?

DADDY (*urging her to cheerfulness*). You remember, Mommy; why we asked ... uh ... what's-her-name to come here?

MRS BARKER. Mrs Barker, if you don't mind.

DADDY. Yes. Mommy? You remember now? About the bumble ... about wanting satisfaction?

MOMMY (*her sorrow turning into delight*). Yes. Why yes! Of course! Yes! Oh, how wonderful!

MRS BARKER (*to the* YOUNG MAN). This is Mommy.

YOUNG MAN. How ... how do you do?

MRS BARKER (*stage whisper*). Her name's Mommy.

YOUNG MAN. How ... how do you do, Mommy?

MOMMY. Well! Hello there!

MRS BARKER (*to the* YOUNG MAN). And that is Daddy.

YOUNG MAN. How do you do, sir?

DADDY. How do you do?

MOMMY (*herself again, circling the* YOUNG MAN, *feeling his arm, poking him*). Yes, sir! Yes, sirree! Now this is more like it. Now this is a great deal more like it! Daddy! Come see. Come see if this isn't a great deal more like it.

DADDY. I ... I can see from here, Mommy. It does look a great deal more like it.

MOMMY. Yes, sir. Yes sirree! Mrs Barker, I don't know *how* to thank you.

MRS BARKER. Oh, don't worry about that. I'll send you a bill in the mail.

MOMMY. What this really calls for is a celebration. It calls for a drink.

MRS BARKER. Oh, what a nice idea.

MOMMY. There's some sauterne in the kitchen.

YOUNG MAN. I'll go.

MOMMY. Will you? Oh, how nice. The kitchen's through the archway there.
(as the YOUNG MAN *exits: to* MRS BARKER —)
He's very nice. Really top notch; much better than the other one.

MRS BARKER. I'm glad you're pleased. And I'm glad everything's all straightened out.

MOMMY. Well, at least we know why we sent for you. We're glad that's cleared up. By the way, what's his name?

MRS BARKER. Ha! Call him whatever you like. He's yours. Call him what you called the other one.

MOMMY. Daddy? What did we call the other one?

DADDY (*puzzles*). Why ...

YOUNG MAN (*re-entering with a tray on which are a bottle of sauterne and five glasses*). Here we are!

MOMMY. Hooray! Hooray!

MRS BARKER. Oh, good!

MOMMY (*moving to the tray*). So, let's — Five glasses? Why five? There are only four of us. Why five?

YOUNG MAN (*catches* GRANDMA's *eye;* GRANDMA *indicates she is not there*). Oh, I'm sorry.

MOMMY. You must learn to count. We're a wealthy family, and you must learn to count.

YOUNG MAN. I will.

MOMMY. Well, everybody take a glass.
(*They do.*)

And we'll drink to celebrate. To satisfaction! Who says you can't get satisfaction these days!

MRS BARKER. What dreadful sauterne!

MOMMY. Yes, isn't it?

(*to* YOUNG MAN, *her voice already a little fuzzy from the wine*)

You don't know how happy I am to see you! Yes sirree. Listen, that time we had with ... with the other one. I'll tell you about it some time.

(*Indicates* MRS BARKER.)

After she's gone. She was responsible for all the trouble in the first place. I'll tell you all about it.

(*Sidles up to him a little.*)

Maybe ... maybe later tonight.

YOUNG MAN (*not moving away*). Why yes. That would be very nice.

MOMMY (*puzzles*). Something familiar about you ... you know that? I can't quite place it....

GRANDMA (*interrupting ... to audience*). Well, I guess that just about wraps it up. I mean, for better or worse, this is a comedy, and I don't think we'd better go any further. No, definitely not. So, let's leave things as they are right now ... while everybody's happy ... while everybody's got what he wants ... or everybody's got what he thinks he wants. Good night, dears.

CURTAIN

THE DEATH OF BESSIE SMITH

A Play in Eight Scenes (1959)

for

NED ROREM

FIRST PERFORMANCE: April 21st, 1960. Berlin, Germany. Schlosspark Theater.

THE DEATH OF BESSIE SMITH

The Players:

BERNIE: A Negro, about forty, thin.

JACK: A dark-skinned Negro, forty-five, bulky, with a deep
    voice and a moustache.

THE FATHER: A thin, balding white man, about fifty-five.

THE NURSE: A southern white girl, full-blown, dark or red-
    haired, pretty, with a wild laugh. Twenty-six.

THE ORDERLY: A light-skinned Negro, twenty-eight, clean-
    shaven, trim, prim.

SECOND NURSE: A southern white girl, blonde, not too
    pretty, about thirty.

THE INTERN: A southern white man, blond, well-put-together,
    with an amiable face; thirty.

*Afternoon and early evening, September 26th, 1937. In and around
the city of Memphis, Tennessee.*

*The set for this play will vary, naturally, as stages vary — from
theatre to theatre. So, the suggestions put down below, while they
might serve as a useful guide, are but a general idea — what the
author 'sees'.*

*What the author 'sees' is this: The central and front area of the
stage reserved for the admissions room of a hospital, for this is where
the major portion of the action of the play takes place. The admissions desk and chair stage-centre, facing the audience. A door,
leading outside, stage-right; a door leading to further areas of the
hospital, stage-left. Very little more: a bench, perhaps; a chair or
two. Running along the rear of the stage, and perhaps a bit on the*

sides, there should be a raised platform, on which, at various locations, against just the most minimal suggestions of sets, the other scenes of the play are performed. All of this very open, for the whole back wall of the stage is full of the sky, which will vary from scene to scene: a hot blue; a sunset; a great, red-orange-yellow sunset. Sometimes full, sometimes but a hint.

At the curtain, let the entire stage be dark against the sky, which is a hot blue. Music against this, for a moment or so, fading to under as the lights come up on:

Scene 1

The corner of a barroom. BERNIE *seated at a table, a beer before him, with glass.* JACK *enters, tentatively, a beer bottle in his hand; he does not see* BERNIE.

BERNIE (*recognizing* JACK; *with pleased surprise*). Hey!

JACK. Hm?

BERNIE. Hey; Jack!

JACK. Hm? ... What? ... (*Recognizes him.*) Bernie!

BERNIE. What you doin' here, boy? C'mon, sit down.

JACK. Well, I'll be damned....

BERNIE. C'mon, sit down, Jack.

JACK. Yeah ... sure ... well, I'll be damned. (*Moves over to the table; sits.*) Bernie. My God, it's hot. How you been, boy?

BERNIE. Fine; fine. What you *doin'* here?

JACK. Oh, travellin'; travellin'.

BERNIE. On the move, hunh? Boy, you are the last person I expected t'walk in that door; small world, hunh?

JACK. Yeah; yeah.

BERNIE. On the move, hunh? Where you goin'?

JACK (*almost, but not quite, mysterious*). North.

BERNIE (*laughs*). North! North? That's a big place, friend: north.

JACK. Yeah … yeah, it is that: a big place.

BERNIE (*after a pause; laughs again*). Well, *where*, boy? North *where*?

JACK (*coyly; proudly*). New York.

BERNIE. New York!

JACK. Unh-hunh; unh-hunh.

BERNIE. New York, hunh? Well. What you got goin' up there?

JACK (*coy again*). Oh … well … I got somethin' goin' up there. What *you* been up to, boy?

BERNIE. New York, hunh?

JACK (*obviously dying to tell about it*). Unh-hunh.

BERNIE (*knowing it*). Well, now, isn't that somethin'. Hey! You want a beer? You want another beer?

JACK. No, I gotta get … well, I don't know, I …

BERNIE (*rising from the table*). Sure you do. Hot like this? You need a beer or two, cool you off.

JACK (*settling back*). Yeah; why not? Sure, Bernie.

BERNIE (*a dollar bill in his hand; moving off*). I'll get us a pair. New York, hunh? What's it all about, Jack? Hunh?

JACK (*chuckles*). Ah, you'd be surprised, boy; you'd be surprised.

(*Lights fade on this scene, come up on another, which is —*)

Scene 2

Part of a screened-in porch; some wicker furniture, a little the worse for wear.

The Nurse's FATHER *is seated on the porch, a cane by his chair. Music, loud, from a phonograph, inside.*

FATHER (*the music is too loud; he grips the arms of his chair; finally —*). Stop it! Stop it! Stop it! Stop it!

NURSE (*from inside*). What? What did you say?

FATHER. STOP IT!

NURSE (*appearing, dressed for duty*). I can't hear you; what do you want?

FATHER. Turn it off! Turn that goddam music off!

NURSE. Honestly, Father ...

FATHER. Turn it off!

(*The* NURSE *turns wearily, goes back inside. Music stops.*) Goddam nigger records. (*to* NURSE, *inside*) I got a headache.

NURSE (*re-entering*). What?

FATHER. I said, I got a headache; you play those goddam records all the time; blast my head off; you play those goddam nigger records full blast ... me with a headache ...

NURSE (*wearily*). You take your pill?

FATHER. No!

NURSE (*turning*). I'll get you your pills....

FATHER. I don't want 'em!

NURSE (*over-patiently*). All right; then I won't get you your pills.

FATHER (*after a pause; quietly, petulantly*). You play those goddam records all the time....

NURSE (*impatiently*). I'm sorry, Father; I didn't know you had your headache.

FATHER. Don't you use that tone with me!

NURSE (*with that tone*). I wasn't using any tone....

FATHER. Don't argue!

NURSE. I am not arguing; I don't *want* to argue; it's too *hot* to argue. (*Pause; then quietly —*) I don't see why a person can't play a couple of records around here without ...

FATHER. Damn noise! That's all it is; damn noise.

NURSE (*after a pause*). I don't suppose you'll drive me to work. I don't suppose, with your headache, you feel up to driving me to the hospital.

FATHER. No.

NURSE. I didn't think you would. And I suppose *you're* going to need the car, too.

FATHER. Yes.

NURSE. Yes; I figured you would. What are you going to do, Father? Are you going to sit here all afternoon on the porch, with your headache, and *watch* the car? Are you going to sit here and watch it all afternoon? You going to sit here with a shotgun and make sure the birds don't crap on it ... or something?

FATHER. I'm going to need it.

NURSE. Yeah; sure.

FATHER. I said, I'm going to need it.

NURSE. Yeah ... I heard you. You're going to need it.

FATHER. I am!

NURSE. Yeah; no doubt. You going to drive down to the Democratic Club, and sit around with that bunch of loafers? You going to play big politician today? Hunh?

FATHER. That's enough, now.

NURSE. You going to go down there with that bunch of bums ... light up one of those expensive cigars, which you have no business smoking, which you can't afford, which *I* cannot afford, to put it more accurately ... the same brand His Honour the mayor smokes ... you going to sit down there and talk big, about how you and the mayor are like *this* ... you going to pretend you're something more than you really are, which is nothing but ...

FATHER. You be quiet, you!

NURSE. ... a hanger-on ... a flunkey ...

FATHER. YOU BE QUIET!

NURSE (*faster*). Is that what you need the car for, Father, and I am going to have to take that hot, stinking bus to the hospital?

FATHER. I said quiet! (*Pause.*) I'm sick and tired of hearing you disparage my friendship with the mayor.

NURSE (*contemptuous*). Friendship!

FATHER. That's right: friendship.

NURSE. I'll tell you what I'll do: Now that we have His Honour, the mayor, as a patient ... when I get down to the hospital ... if I ever get there on that damn bus ... I'll pay him a call, and I'll just *ask* him about your 'friendship' with him; I'll just ...

FATHER. Don't you go disturbing him; you hear me?

NURSE. Why, I should think the mayor would be de*light*ed if the daughter of one of his closest friends was to ...

FATHER. You're going to make trouble!

NURSE (*heavily sarcastic*). Oh, how could I make trouble, Father?

FATHER. You be careful.

NURSE. Oh, that must be quite a friendship. Hey, I got a good idea: you could drive me down to the hospital and you could pay a visit to your good friend the mayor at the same time. Now, *that* is a good idea.

FATHER. Leave off! Just leave off!

NURSE (*under her breath*). You make me sick.

FATHER. What! What was that?

NURSE (*very quietly*). I said, you make me sick, Father.

FATHER. Yeah? Yeah?

(*He takes his cane, raps it against the floor several times. This gesture, beginning in anger, alters, as it becomes weaker, to a helpless and pathetic flailing; eventually it subsides; the* NURSE *watches it all quietly.*)

NURSE (*tenderly*). Are you done?

FATHER. Go away; go to work.

NURSE. I'll get you your pills before I go.

FATHER (*tonelessly*). I said, I don't want them.

NURSE. I don't care whether you *want* them, or not....

FATHER. I'm not one of your patients!

NURSE. Oh, and aren't I glad you're not.

FATHER. You give them better attention than you give me!

NURSE (*wearily*). I don't have patients, Father; I am not a floor nurse; will you get that into your head? I am on admissions; I am on the admissions desk. You *know* that; why do you pretend otherwise?

FATHER. If you were a ... what-do-you-call-it ... if you were a floor nurse ... if you *were*, you'd give your patients better attention than you give me.

NURSE. What *are* you, Father? What are you? Are you sick, or not? Are you a ... a ... a poor cripple, or are you planning to get yourself up out of that chair, after I go to work, and drive yourself down to the Democratic Club and sit around with that bunch of loafers? Make up your mind, Father; you can't have it every which way.

FATHER. Never mind.

NURSE. You can't; you just can't.

FATHER. Never mind, now!

NURSE (*after a pause*). Well, I gotta get to work.

FATHER (*sneering*). Why don't you get your boy-friend to drive you to work?

NURSE. All right; leave off.

FATHER. Why don't you get him to come by and pick you up, hunh?

NURSE. I said, leave off!

FATHER. Or is he only interested in driving you back here at night ... when it's nice and dark; when it's plenty dark for messing around in his car? Is that it? Why don't you bring him here and let *me* have a look at him; why don't you let me get a look at him some time?

NURSE (*angry*). Well, Father ... (*a very brief gesture at the*

surroundings) maybe it's because I don't want him to get
a ...

FATHER. I hear you; I hear you at night; I hear you gigglin' and
carrying on out there in his car; I hear you!

NURSE (*loud; to cover the sound of his voice*). I'm going, Father.

FATHER. All right; get along, then; get on!

NURSE. You're damned right!

FATHER. Go on! Go!

(*The* NURSE *regards him for a moment; turns, exits.*)
And don't stay out there all night in his car, when you get
back. You hear me? (*Pause.*) You hear me?
(*Lights fade on this scene; come up on* —)

Scene 3

A bare area. JACK *enters, addresses his remarks off-stage and to an
invisible mirror on an invisible dresser. Music under this scene, as
though coming from a distance.*

JACK. Hey ... Bessie! C'mon, now. Hey ... honey? Get your
butt out of bed ... wake up. C'mon; the goddam afternoon's half gone; we gotta get movin'. Hey ... I called
that son-of-a-bitch in New York ... *I* told him, all right.
I told him what you said. Wake up, baby, we gotta get out
of this dump; I gotta get you to Memphis 'fore seven
o'clock ... and then ... POW! ... *we* are headin' straight
north. Here we come; NEW YORK. I told that bastard ...
I said: Look, you don't have no exclusive rights on
Bessie ... nobody's got 'em ... Bessie is doin' you a favour
... she's doin' you a goddam favour. She don't *have* to sing
for you. I said: Bessie's tired ... she don't wanna travel now.
An' he said: You don't *wanna* back out of this ... Bessie
told me *herself* ... and I said: Look ... don't worry yourself
... Bessie said she'd cut more sides for you ... she will ...

she'll make all the goddam new records you want....
What I mean to say *is*, just don't you get any ideas about
havin' exclusive rights ... because nobody's got 'em.
(*Giggles.*) I told him you was free as a bird, honey. Free as a
goddam bird. (*Looks in at her, shakes his head.*) Some bird!
I been downstairs to check us out. I go downstairs to
check us out, and I run into a friend of mine ... and we sit
in the bar and have a few, and he says: What're *you* doin'
now; what're you doin' in this crummy hotel? And I say:
I am cartin' a bird around with me. I'm cartin' her north; I
got a fat lady upstairs; she is sleepin' off last night. An' he
says: You always got *some* fat lady upstairs, somewhere;
boy, I never seen it fail. An' I say: This ain't just no plain
fat lady I got upstairs ... this is a celebrity, boy ... this is a
rich old fat singin' lady ... an' he laughed an' he said:
Boy, who you got up there? I say: You guess. An' he says:
C'mon ... I can't *guess*. An' I told him ... I am travellin'
with Miss Bessie Smith. An' he looked at me, an' he said,
real quiet: Jesus, boy, are you travellin' with Bessie?
An' I said ... an' real proud: You're damn right I'm
travellin' with Bessie. An' he want to meet you; so you get
your big self out of bed; we're goin' to go downstairs,
'cause I wanna show you off. C'mon, now; I mean I *gotta*
show you off. 'Cause then he said: Whatever *happened*
to Bessie? An' I said: What do you mean, whatever
happened to Bessie? She's right upstairs. An' he said: I
mean, what's she been doin' the past four-five years?
There was a time there, boy, Chicago an' all, New York,
she was the hottest goddam thing goin'. Is she still singin'?
YOU HEAR THAT? That's what he said: Is she still
singin'? An' I said ... I said, you been tired ... you been
restin'. You ain't been forgotten, honey, but they are
askin' questions. SO YOU GET UP! We're drivin' north

tonight, an' when you get in New York ... *you* show 'em where you been. Honey, you're gonna go back on top again ... I mean it ... you *are*. I'm gonna get you up to New York. 'Cause you gotta make that date. I mean, sure, baby, you're free as a goddam bird, an' I did tell that son-of-a-bitch he don't have exclusive rights on you ... but, honey ... he *is* interested ... an' you gotta hustle for it now. You do; 'cause if you don't do *somethin'*, people are gonna stop askin' where you been the past four-five years ... they're gonna stop askin' anything at all! You hear? An' if I say downstairs you're rich ... that don't make it so, Bessie. No more, honey. You gotta make this goddam trip ... you gotta get goin' again. (*pleading*) Baby? Honey? You know I'm not lyin' to you. C'mon now; get up. We go downstairs to the bar an' have a few ... see my friend ... an' then we'll get in that car ... and *go*. 'Cause it's gettin' late, honey ... it's gettin' awful late. (*brighter*) Hey! You awake? (*moving to the wings*) Well, c'mon, then, Bessie ... let's get up. We're goin' north again!

(*The lights fade on this scene. Music.*
The sunset is predominant.)

JACK (*off stage*). Ha, ha; thanks; thanks a lot. (*Car door slams. Car motor starts.*) O.K.; here we go; we're on our way. (*Sound of car motor gunning, car moving off, fading.*)

(*The sunset dims again.*
Music, fading, as the lights come up on —)

Scene 4

The admissions room of the hospital. The NURSE *is at her desk; the* ORDERLY *stands to one side.*

ORDERLY. The mayor of Memphis! I went into his room and there he was; the mayor of Memphis. Lying right there, flat on his belly ... a cigar in his mouth ... an unlit cigar stuck in his mouth, chewing on it, chewing on a big, unlit cigar ... shuffling a lot of papers in his hands, a pillow shoved up under his chest to give him some freedom for all those papers ... and I came in, and I said: Good afternoon, Your Honour ... and he swung his face round and he looked at me and he shouted: My ass hurts, you get the hell out of here!

NURSE (*laughs freely*). His Honour has got his ass in a sling, and that's for sure.

ORDERLY. And I got out; I left very quickly; I closed the door fast.

NURSE. The mayor and his haemorrhoids ... the mayor's late haemorrhoids ... are a matter of deep concern to this institution, for the mayor built this hospital; the mayor is here with his ass in a sling, and the seat of government is now in Room 206 ... so you be nice and respectful. (*Laughs.*) There is a man two rooms down who walked in here last night after you went off ... that man walked in here with his hands over his gut to keep his insides from spilling right out on this desk ...

ORDERLY. I heard....

NURSE. ... and that man may live, or he may not live, and the wagers are heavy that he will not live ... but we are not one bit more concerned for that man than we are for His Honour ... no sir.

ORDERLY (*chuckling*). I like your contempt.

NURSE. You what? You like my *contempt*, do you? Well now, don't misunderstand me. Just what do you think I meant? What have you got it in your mind that I was saying?

ORDERLY. Why, it's a matter of proportion. Surely you don't *condone* the fact that the mayor and his piles, and that poor man lying up there ... ?

NURSE. *Condone!* Will you listen to that: condone! My!

THE DEATH OF BESSIE SMITH

Aren't you the educated one? What ... what does that
word mean, boy? That word condone? Hunh? You do
talk some, don't you? You have a great deal to learn.
Now it's true that the poor man lying up there with his
guts coming out could be a nigger for all the attention he'd
get if His Honour should start shouting for something ...
he could be on the operating table ... and they'd drop his
insides right on the floor and come running if the mayor
should want his cigar lit.... But that is the way things *are*.
Those are facts. You had better acquaint yourself with
some realities.

ORDERLY. I know ... I know the mayor is an important man.
He *is* impressive ... even lying on his belly like he is....
I'd like to get to talk to him.

NURSE. Don't you know it! TALK to him! Talk to the mayor?
What for?

ORDERLY. I've told you. I've told you I don't intend to stay here
carrying crap pans and washing out the operating theatre
until I have a ... a long grey beard ... I'm ... I'm going
beyond that.

NURSE (*patronizing*). Sure.

ORDERLY. *I've* told you ... I'm going beyond that. This ...

NURSE (*shakes her head in amused disbelief*). Oh, my. Listen ...
you should count yourself lucky, boy. Just what do you
think is going to happen to you? Is His Honour, the mayor,
going to rise up out of his sick-bed and take a personal
interest in you? Write a letter to the President, maybe?
And is Mr Roosevelt going to send his wife, Lady Eleanor,
down here after you? Or is it in your plans that you are
going to be handed a big fat scholarship somewhere to
the north of Johns Hopkins? Boy, you just don't know!
I'll tell you something ... you are lucky as you are.
Whatever do you expect?

THE DEATH OF BESSIE SMITH

ORDERLY. What's been promised.... Nothing more. Just that.

NURSE. Promised! Promised? Oh, boy, I'll tell you about promises. Don't you know yet that everything is promises ... and that is all there is to it? Promises ... nothing more! I am personally sick of promises. Would you like to hear a little poem? Would you like me to recite some verse for you? Here is a little poem: 'You kiss the niggers and I'll kiss the Jews and we'll stay in the White House as long as we choose.' And that ... according to what I am told ... that is what Mr and Mrs Roosevelt sit at the breakfast table and sing to each other over their orange juice, right in the White House. Promises, boy! Promises ... and that is what they are going to stay.

ORDERLY. There are *some* people who believe in more than promises....

NURSE. Hunh?

ORDERLY (*cautious now*). I say, there are some people who believe in more than promises; there are some people who believe in action.

NURSE. What's that? What did you say?

ORDERLY. Action ... ac — ... Never mind.

NURSE (*her eyes narrow*). No ... no, go on now ... action? What kind of action do you mean?

ORDERLY. *I* don't *mean* anything ... all I said was ...

NURSE. I heard you. You know ... I know what you been doing. You been listening to the great white doctor again ... that big, good-looking blond intern you *admire* so much because he is so liberal-thinking, eh? My suitor? (*Laughs.*) My suitor ... my very own white knight, who is wasting his time patching up decent folk right here when there is dying going on in Spain. (*exaggerated*) Oh, there is dying in Spain. And he is held here! That's who you have been listening to.

ORDERLY. I don't mean that .... I don't pay any attention ... (*weakly*) to that kind of talk. I do my job here ... I try to keep ...

NURSE (*contemptuous*). You try to keep yourself on the good side of everybody, don't you, boy? You stand there and you nod your kinky little head and say yes'm, yes'm, at everything I say, and then when he's here you go off in a corner and you get him and you sympathize with him ... you get him to tell you about ... promises! ... and ... and ... action! ... I'll tell you right now, he's going to get himself into trouble ... and you're helping him right along.

ORDERLY. No, now. I don't ...

NURSE (*with some disgust*). All that talk of his! Action! I know all what he talks about ... like about that bunch of radicals came through here last spring ... causing the rioting ... that arson! Stuff like that. Didn't ... didn't you have someone get banged up in that?

ORDERLY (*contained*). My uncle got run down by a lorry full of state police ...

NURSE. ... which the Governor called out because of the rioting ... and that arson! Action! That was a fine bunch of action. Is that what you mean? Is that what you get him off in a corner and get him to talk about ... and pretend you're interested? Listen, boy ... if you're going to get yourself in with those folks, you'd better ...

ORDERLY (*quickly*). I'm not mixed up with any folks ... honestly ... I'm not. I just want to ...

NURSE. I'll tell you what you just want.... I'll tell you what you just want if you have any mind to keep this good job you've got.... You just shut your ears ... and you keep that mouth closed tight, too. All this talk about what you are going to go beyond! You keep walking a real tight line here, and ... and at night ... (*She begins to giggle.*)

74

... and at night, if you want to, on your own time ... at night you keep right on putting that bleach on your hands and your neck and your face ...

ORDERLY. I do no such thing!

NURSE (*in full laughter*). ... and you keep right on bleaching away ... b-l-e-a-c-h-i-n-g a-w-a-y ... but you do that on your own time ... you can do all that on your own time.

ORDERLY (*pleading*). I do no such thing!

NURSE. The hell you don't! You are such a ...

ORDERLY. That kind of talk is very ...

NURSE. ... you are so mixed up! You are going to be one funny sight. You, over there in a corner playing up to him ... well, boy, you are going to be one funny sight come the millennium.... The great black mob marching down the street, banners in the air ... that great black mob ... and you right there in the middle, your bleached-out, snowy-white face in the middle of the pack like that ... (*She breaks down in laughter.*) ... oh ... oh, my ... oh. I tell you, that will be quite a sight.

ORDERLY (*plaintive*). I wish you'd stop that.

NURSE. Quite a sight.

ORDERLY. I wish you wouldn't make fun of me ... I don't give you any cause.

NURSE. Oh, my ... oh, I *am* sorry ... I am *so* sorry.

ORDERLY. I don't think I give you any cause....

NURSE. You don't, eh?

ORDERLY. No.

NURSE. Well ... you *are* a true little gentleman, that's for sure ... you *are* polite ... and deferential ... and you are a genuine little ass-licker, if I ever saw one. Tell me, boy ...

ORDERLY (*stiffening a little*). There is no need ...

NURSE (*maliciously solicitous*). Tell me, boy ... is it true that you have Uncle Tom'd yourself right out of the bosom of your family ... right out of your circle of acquaintances? Is it true, young man, that you are now an inhabitant of no-man's-land, on the one side shunned and disowned by your brethren, and on the other an object of contempt and derision to your betters? Is that your problem, son?

ORDERLY. You ... you shouldn't do that. I ... work hard ... I try to advance myself ... I give nobody trouble.

NURSE. I'll tell you what you do.... You go north, boy ... you go up to New York City, where nobody's any better than anybody else ... get up north, boy. (*Abrupt change of tone.*) But before you do anything like that, you run on downstairs and get me a pack of cigarettes.

ORDERLY (*pauses; is about to speak; thinks better of it; moves off to door, rear*). Yes'm.

(*Exits. The* NURSE *watches him leave. After he is gone, she shakes her head, laughs, parodies him.*)

NURSE. Yes'm ... yes'm ... ha, ha, ha! You white niggers kill me.

(*She picks up her desk phone, dials a number, as the lights come up on —*)

Scene 5

The scene is both the hospital set of the preceding scene and, as well, on the raised platform, another admissions desk of another hospital. The desk is empty. The phone rings, twice. The SECOND NURSE *comes in, slowly, filing her nails, maybe.*

SECOND NURSE (*lazily answering the phone*). Mercy Hospital.
NURSE. Mercy Hospital! Mercy, indeed, you away from your desk all the time. *Some* hospitals are run better than *others; some* nurses stay at their posts.

SECOND NURSE (*bored*). Oh, hi. What do you want?
NURSE. I don't *want* anything....

SECOND NURSE (*pause*). Oh. Well, what did you call for?

NURSE. I didn't call *for* anything. I (*shrugs*) just called.

SECOND NURSE. Oh.

    (*The lights dim a little on the two nurses.*)

    (*Music.*
    Car sounds up.)

JACK (*off stage, laughing*). I tell you, honey, he didn't like that. No, sir, he didn't. You comfortable, honey. Hunh? You just lean back and enjoy the ride, baby; we're makin' good time. Yes, we are makin'… WATCH OUT! WATCH…

    (*Sound of crash.… Silence.*)

Honey … baby … we have crashed … you all right? … BESSIE! BESSIE!

    (*Music up again —*)

    (*— fading as the lights come up full again on the two nurses.*)

NURSE. … and, what else? Oh, yeah; *we* have got the mayor here.

SECOND NURSE. That's nice. What's he doin'?

NURSE. He isn't *doin'* anything; he is a patient here.

SECOND NURSE. Oh. Well, *we* had the mayor's wife *here* … last April.

NURSE. Unh-hunh. Well, *we* got the mayor *here*, now.

SECOND NURSE (*very bored*). Unh-hunh. Well, that's nice.

NURSE (*turns, sees the* INTERN *entering*). Oh, lover-boy just walked in; I'll call you later, hunh?

SECOND NURSE. Unh-hunh.

    (*They both hang up. The lights fade on the* SECOND NURSE.)

Scene 6

NURSE. Well, how is the Great White Doctor this evening?

INTERN (*irritable*). Oh … drop it.

NURSE. Oh, my ... where is your cheerful demeanour this evening, Doctor?

INTERN (*smiling in spite of himself*). How do you do it? How do you manage to just dismiss things from your mind? How can you say a ... cheerful hello to someone ... dismissing from your mind ... excusing yourself for the vile things you have said the evening before?

NURSE (*lightly*). I said nothing vile. I put you in your place ... that's all. I ... I merely put you in your place ... as I have done before ... and as I shall do again.

INTERN (*is about to say something; thinks better of it; sighs*). Never mind ... forget about it ... Did you *see* the sunset?

NURSE (*mimicking*). No, I didn't *see* the sunset. *What* is it doing?

INTERN (*amused; puts it on heavily*). The west is burning ... fire has enveloped fully half of the continent ... the ... the fingers of the flame stretch upward to the stars ... and ... and there is a monstrous burning circumference hanging on the edge of the world.

NURSE (*laughs*). Oh, my ... oh, my.

INTERN (*serious*). It's a truly beautiful sight. Go out and have a look.

NURSE (*coquettish*). Oh, Doctor, I am chained to my desk of pain, so I must rely on you.... Talk the sunset to me, you ... you monstrous burning intern hanging on the edge of my circumference ... ha, ha, *ha*.

INTERN (*leans towards her*). When?

NURSE. When?

INTERN (*lightly*). When ... when are you going to let me nearer, woman?

NURSE. Oh, my!

INTERN. Here am I ... here am I tangential, while all the while I would serve more nobly as a radiant, not outward from, but reversed, plunging straight to your lovely vortex.

NURSE (*laughs*). Oh, la! You must keep your mind off my lovely vortex ... you just remain ... uh ... tangential.

INTERN (*mock despair*). *How* is a man to fulfil himself? Here I offer you love ... consider the word ... love.... Here I offer you my love, my self ... my bored bed ...

NURSE. I note your offer ... your offer is noted. (*Holds out a clipboard.*) Here ... do you want your reports?

INTERN. No ... I don't want my reports. Give them here. (*Takes the clip-board.*)

NURSE. And while you're here with your hot breath on me, hand me a cigarette. I sent the nigger down for a pack. I ran out. (*He gives her a cigarette.*) Match?

INTERN. Go light it on the sunset. (*Tosses match to her.*) He says you owe him for three packs.

NURSE (*lights her cigarette*). Your bored bed ... indeed.

INTERN. Ma'am ... the heart yearns, the body burns ...

NURSE. And *I* haven't time for *interns*.

INTERN. ... the heart yearns, the body burns ... and I haven't time ... Oh, I don't know ... the things you women can do to art.

(*More intimate, but still light.*)

Have you told your father, yet? Have you told your father that I am hopelessly in love with you? Have you told him that at night the sheets of my bed are like a tent, poled centre-upward in my love for you?

NURSE (*wry*). I'll tell him ... I'll tell my father just that ... just what you said ... and he'll be down here after you for talking to a young lady like that! Really!

INTERN. My God! I forgot myself! A cloistered maiden in whose house trousers are never mentioned ... in which flies, I am sure, are referred to only as winged bugs. Here I thought I was talking to someone, to a certain young nurse, whose collection of anatomical jokes for all occasions ...

NURSE (*giggles*). Oh, you be still, now. (*lofty*) Besides, just because I play coarse and flip around here ... to keep my place with the rest of you ... don't you think for a minute that I relish this turn to the particular from the general.... If you don't mind, we'll just cease this talk.

INTERN (*half sung*). I'm always in tumescence for you. You'd never guess the things I ...

NURSE (*blush-giggle*). Now stop that! Really, I mean it!

INTERN. Then marry me, woman. If nothing else, marry me.

NURSE. Don't, now.

INTERN (*joking and serious at the same time*). Marry me.

NURSE (*matter-of-fact, but not unkindly*). I am sick of this talk. My poor father may have some funny ideas; he may be having a pretty hard time reconciling himself to things as they are. But not me! Forty-six dollars a month! Isn't that right? Isn't that what you make? Forty-six dollars a month! Boy, you can't afford even to think about marrying. You can't afford marriage.... Best you can afford is lust. That's the best you can afford.

INTERN (*scathing*). Oh ... gentle woman ... nineteenth-century lady out of place in this vulgar time ... maiden versed in petit point and murmured talk of the weather ...

NURSE. Now I mean it ... you can cut that talk right out.

INTERN. ... type my great-grandfather fought and died for ... forty-six dollars a month and the best I can afford is lust! Jesus, woman!

NURSE. All right ... you can quit making fun of me. You can quit it right this minute.

INTERN. *I*! Making fun of *you* ... !

NURSE. I am tired of being toyed with; I am tired of your impractical propositions. Must you dwell on what is not going to happen? Must you ask me, constantly, over and over again, the same question to which you are already

aware you will get the same answer? Do you get pleasure
from it? What unreasonable form of contentment do you
derive from persisting in this?

INTERN (*lightly*). Because I love you?

NURSE. Oh, that would help matters along; it really would ...
even if it were *true*. The economic realities would pick
up their skirts, whoop, and depart before the lance-high,
love-smit knight. My knight, whose real and true interest,
if we come right down to it, as indicated in the order of
your propositions, is, and always has been, a convenient
and uncomplicated bedding down.

INTERN (*smiling, and with great gallantry*). I have offered to
marry you.

NURSE. Yeah ... sure ... you have offered to marry me. The
United States is chuck-full of girls who have heard that
great promise — I will marry you ... I will marry you
... IF! If! The great promise with its great conditional
attached to it....

INTERN (*amused*). Who are you pretending to be?

NURSE (*abrupt*). What do you mean?

INTERN (*laughing*). Oh, *nothing*.

NURSE (*regards him silently for a moment; then —*). Marry me! Do
you know ... do you know that nigger I sent to fetch me
a pack of butts ... do you know he is in a far better
position ... realistically, economically ... to ask to marry
me than you are? Hunh? Do you know that? That nigger!
Do you know that nigger outearns you ... and by a *lot*?

INTERN (*bows to her*). I know he does ... and I know what value
you, you and your famous family, put on such things.
So, I have an idea for you ... why don't you just *ask*
that nigger to marry you? 'Cause, boy, he'd never ask
you! I'm sure if you told your father about it, it would
give him some pause at first, because we know what type

of man your father is ... don't we? ... But then he would think about it ... and realize the advantages of the match ... realistically ... economically ... and he would find some way to adjust his values, in consideration of your happiness, and security....

NURSE (*flicks her still-lit cigarette at him, hard; hits him with it*). You are disgusting!

INTERN. Damn you, bitch!

NURSE. Disgusting!

INTERN. Realistic ... practical.... (*a little softer, now*) Your family is a famous *name*, but those thousand acres are *gone*, and the pillars of your house are blistered and flaking.... (*harder*) Not that your family ever *had*, within human memory, a thousand acres to *go* ... *or* a house with pillars in the first place....

NURSE (*angry*). I am fully aware of what is true and what is not true. (*soberly*) Go about your work and leave me be.

INTERN (*sweetly*). Aw.

NURSE. I said ... leave me be.

INTERN (*brushing himself*). It is a criminal offence to set fire to interns ... orderlies you may burn at will, unless you have other plans for them ... but interns ...

NURSE. ... are a dime a dozen. (*Giggles.*) Did I burn you?

INTERN. No, you did not burn me.

NURSE. That's too bad ... would have served you right if I had. (*Pauses; then smiles.*) I'm sorry, honey.

INTERN (*mock formal*). I accept your apology ... and I await your surrender.

NURSE (*laughs*). Well, you just await it. (*A pause.*) Hey, what are you going to do about the mayor being here now?

INTERN. What am I supposed to do about it? I am on emergencies, and he is not an emergency case.

NURSE. I told you ... I told you what you should do.

82

INTERN. I know ... I should go upstairs to his room ... I should pull up a chair, and I should sit down and I should say, How's tricks, Your Honour?

NURSE. Well, you make fun if you want to ... but if you listen to me, you'll know you need some people *behind* you.

INTERN. Strangers!

NURSE. Strangers don't stay strangers ... not if you don't let them. He could do something for you if he had a mind to.

INTERN. Yes he could ... indeed, he *could* do something for me.... He could give me his car ... he could make me a present of his Cord automobile.... That would be the finest thing any mayor ever did for a private citizen. Have you seen that car?

NURSE. Have I seen that car? Have I seen this ... have I seen that? Cord automobiles and ... and sunsets ... those are ... fine preoccupations. Is that what you think about? Huh? Driving a fine car into a fine sunset?

INTERN (*quietly*). Lord knows, I'd like to get away from here.

NURSE (*nodding*). I know ... I know. Well, maybe you're going to *have* to get away from here. People are aware how dissatisfied you are ... people have heard a lot about your ... dissatisfactions.... My father has heard ... people got wind of the way you feel about things. People here aren't good enough for your attentions.... Foreigners ... a bunch of foreigners who are cutting each other up in their own business ... that's where you'd like to be, isn't it?

INTERN (*quietly; intensely*). There are over half a million people killed in that war! Do you know that? By airplanes.... Civilians! You misunderstand me so! I am ... all right ... this way.... My dissatisfactions ... you call them that ... my dissatisfactions have nothing to do with loyalties.... I am not concerned with politics ... but I have a sense of urgency … a dislike of waste … stagnation … I am *stranded* … *here*…. My talents are not large … but the emergencies of the emergency ward of this second-rate hospital in this second-rate state…. No! … it isn't enough. Oh, you listen to me. If I could … if I could bandage the arm of one person … if I could be over there right this minute … you could take the city of Memphis … you could take the whole state … and don't you forget I was born here … you could take the whole goddam state….

NURSE (*hard*). Well, I have a very good idea of how we could arrange that. I have a dandy idea…. We could just tell the mayor about the way you feel, and he'd be delighted to help you on your way … out of this hospital at the very least, and maybe out of the state! And I don't think he'd be giving you any Cord automobile as a going-away present, either. He'd set you out, all right … he'd set you right out on your *butt*! That's what he'd do.

INTERN (*with a rueful half-smile*). Yes … yes … I imagine he would. I feel lucky … I feel doubly fortunate, now … having you … feeling the way we do about each other.

NURSE. You are so sarcastic!

INTERN. Well, how the hell do you expect me to behave?

NURSE. Just … (*Laughs.*) … oh, boy, this is good … just like I told the nigger … you walk a straight line, and you do your job … (*Turns coy, here.*) … and … and unless you are kept late by some emergency more pressing than your … … (*Smiles wryly.*) … 'love' … for me … I may let you drive me home tonight … in your beat-up Chevvy.

INTERN. Woman, as always I anticipate with enormous pleasure the prospect of driving you home … a stop along the way … fifteen minutes or so of … of tantalizing preliminary love play ending in an infuriating and inconclusive wrestling match, during which you hiss of the … the

84

liberties I should not take, and I sound the horn once or
twice accidentally with my elbow ...

(*She giggles at this.*)

... and, finally, in my beat-up car, in front of your father's
beat-up house ... a kiss of searing intensity ... a hand in the
right place ... briefly ... and your hasty departure within.
I am looking forward to this ritual ... as I always do.

NURSE (*pleased*). Why, thank you.

INTERN. I look forward to this ritual because of how it sets me
apart from other men ...

NURSE. Aw ...

INTERN. ... because I am probably the only white man under
sixty in two counties who has *not* had the pleasure of ...

NURSE. LIAR! You no-account mother-grabbing son of a
nigger!

INTERN (*laughs*). Boy! Watch you go!

NURSE. FILTH! You are filth!

INTERN. I am honest ... an honest man. Let me make you an
honest woman.

NURSE (*steaming ... her rage between her teeth*). You have done it,
boy ... you have played around with me and you have
done it. I am going to get you ... I am going to fix you ...
I am going to see to it that you are *through* here ... do you
understand what I'm telling you?

INTERN. There is no ambiguity in your talk now, honey.

NURSE. You're damn right there isn't.

(*The* ORDERLY *re-enters from stage-rear. The* NURSE *sees
him.*)

Get out of here!

(*But he stands there.*)

Do you hear me? You get the hell out of here! GO!

(*He retreats, exits, to silence.*)

INTERN (*chuckling*). King of the castle. My, you *are* something.

NURSE. Did you get what I was telling you?

INTERN. Why, I heard every word ... every sweet syllable....

NURSE. You have overstepped yourself ... and you are going to wish you hadn't. I'll get my father ... I'll have you done with *myself*.

INTERN (*cautious*). Aw, come on, now.

NURSE. I mean it.

INTERN (*lying badly*). Now look ... you don't think I meant ...

NURSE (*mimicking*). Now you don't think I meant ... (*Laughs broadly.*) Oh, my ... you are the funny one.

> (*Her threat, now, has no fury, but is filled with quiet conviction.*)

I said I'll fix you ... and I will. You just go along with your work ... you do your job ... but what I said ... you keep that burning in the back of your brain. We'll go right along, you and I, and we'll be civil ... and it'll be as though nothing had happened ... nothing at all (*Laughs again.*) Honey, your neck is in the *noose* ... and I have a whip ... and I'll set the horse from under you ... when it pleases me.

INTERN (*wryly*). It's going to be nice around here.

NURSE. Oh, yes it is. I'm going to enjoy it ... I really am.

INTERN. Well ... I'll forget about driving you home tonight....

NURSE. Oh, no ... you will *not* forget about driving me home tonight. You will drive me home *tonight* ... you will drive me home *tonight* ... and *tomorrow* night ... you will see me to my *door* ... you will be my gallant. We will have things between us a little bit the way I am told things *used* to be. You will *court* me, boy, and you will do it *right*!

INTERN (*stares at her for a moment*). You impress me. No matter what else, I've got to admit that.

> (*The* NURSE *laughs wildly at this.*

Music.

The lights on this hospital set fade, and come up on the
SECOND NURSE, *at her desk, for —)*

Scene 7

JACK (*rushing in*). Ma'am, I need help, quick!

SECOND NURSE. What d'you want here?

JACK. There has been an accident, ma'am ... I got an injured
woman outside in my car....

SECOND NURSE. Yeah? Is that so? Well, you sit down and
wait.... You go over there and sit down and wait a while.

JACK. This is an emergency! There has been an accident!

SECOND NURSE. YOU WAIT! You just sit down and wait!

JACK. This woman is badly hurt....

SECOND NURSE. YOU COOL YOUR HEELS!

JACK. Ma'am ... I got Bessie Smith out in that car there....

SECOND NURSE. I DON'T CARE WHO YOU GOT OUT
THERE, NIGGER. YOU COOL YOUR HEELS!
(*Music up.*

*The lights fade on this scene, come up again on the main
hospital scene, on the* NURSE *and the* INTERN, *for —)*

Scene 8

Music fades.

NURSE (*loud*). Hey, nigger ... nigger!
(*The* ORDERLY *re-enters.*)

Give me my cigarettes.

INTERN. I think I'll ...

NURSE. You stay here!
(*The* ORDERLY *hands the nurse the cigarettes, cautious and
attentive to see what is wrong.*)

A person could die for a smoke, the time you take.

What'd you do ... sit downstairs in the can and rest your small, shapely feet ... hunh?

ORDERLY. You told me to ... go back outside ...

NURSE. Before that! What'd you do ... go to the cigarette *factory*? Did you take a quick run up to Winston-Salem for these?

ORDERLY. No ... I ...

NURSE. Skip it. *(to the* INTERN*)* Where? Where were you planning to go?

INTERN *(too formal)*. I beg your pardon?

NURSE. I said ... where did you want to go to? Were you off for coffee?

INTERN. Is that what you want? Now that you have your cigarettes, have you hit upon the idea of having coffee, too? Now that he is back from one errand, are you planning to send me on another?

NURSE *(smiling wickedly)*. Yeah ... I think I'd like that ... keep both of you jumping. I *would* like coffee, and I *would* like you to get it for me. So why don't you just trot right across the hall and get me some? And I like it good and hot ... and strong ...

INTERN. ... and black ... ?

NURSE. Cream! ... and sweet ... and in a hurry!

INTERN. I guess your wish is my command ... hunh?

NURSE. You bet it is!

INTERN *(moves half-way to the door, stage-rear, then pauses)*. I just had a lovely thought ... that maybe some time when you are sitting there at your desk opening mail with that stiletto you use for a letter opener, you might slip and tear open your arm ... then you could come running into the emergency ... and I could be there when you came running in, blood coming out of you like water out of a faucet ... and I could take ahold of your arm ...

88

and just hold it ... just hold it ... and watch it flow ... just hold on to you and watch your blood flow....

NURSE (*grabs up the letter opener ... holds it up*). This? More likely between your ribs!

INTERN (*exiting*). One coffee, lady.

NURSE (*after a moment of silence, throws the letter opener back down on her desk*). I'll take care of him. CRACK! I'll crack that whip. (*to the* ORDERLY) What are you standing there for ... hunh? You like to watch what's going on?

ORDERLY. I'm no voyeur.

NURSE. You what? You like to listen in? You take pleasure in it?

ORDERLY. I said no.

NURSE (*half to herself*). I'll bet you don't. I'll take care of him ... talking to me like that ... I'll crack that whip. Let him just wait.

(*to the* ORDERLY, *now*)

My father says that Francisco Franco is going to be victorious in that war over there ... that he's going to win ... and that it's just wonderful.

ORDERLY. He does?

NURSE. Yes, he does. My father says that Francisco Franco has got them licked, and that they're a bunch of radicals, anyway, and it's all to the good ... just wonderful.

ORDERLY. Is that so?

NURSE. I've told you my father is a ... a historian, so he isn't just anybody. His opinion counts for something special. It *still* counts for something special. He says anybody wants to go over there and get mixed up in that thing has got it coming to him ... whatever happens.

ORDERLY. I'm sure your father is an informed man, and ...

NURSE. What?

ORDERLY. I said ... I said ... I'm sure your father is an informed man, and ... his opinion is to be respected.

NURSE. That's right, boy ... you just jump to it and say what you think people want to hear ... you be both sides of the coin. Did you ... did you hear him threaten me there? Did you?

ORDERLY. Oh, now ... I don't think ...

NURSE (*steely*). You heard him threaten me!

ORDERLY. I don't think ...

NURSE. For such a smart boy ... you are so dumb. I don't know what I am going to do with you.

(*She is thinking of the* INTERN *now, and her expression shows it.*)

You refuse to comprehend things, and that bodes badly ... it does. Especially considering it is all but arranged ...

ORDERLY. What is all but arranged?

NURSE (*a great laugh, but mirthless; she is barely under control*). Why, don't you know, boy? Didn't you know that you and I are practically engaged?

ORDERLY. I ... I don't ...

NURSE. Don't you know about the economic realities? Haven't you been apprised of the way things *are*? (*She giggles.*) Our knights are gone forth into sunsets ... behind the wheels of Cord cars ... the acres have diminished and the paint is flaking ... that there is a great ... *abandonment*?

ORDERLY (*cautious*). I don't understand you....

NURSE. No kidding? (*Her voice shakes.*) No kidding ... you don't understand me? Why? What's the matter, boy, don't you get the idea?

ORDERLY (*contained, but angry*). I think you'd tire of riding me some day. I think you *would*....

NURSE. You go up to Room 206, right now ... you go up and tell the mayor that when his butt's better we have a marrying job for him.

ORDERLY (*with some distaste*). Really ... you go much too far....

NURSE. Oh, I do, do I? Well, let me tell you something ... I am sick of it! I am *sick*. I am sick of everything in this hot, stupid, fly-ridden *world*. I am sick of the disparity between things as they are, and as they should be! I am sick of this desk ... this uniform ... it scratches.... I am sick of the sight of *you* ... the *thought* of you makes me ... *itch* ... I am sick of *him*. (*Soft now: a chant.*) I am sick of talking to people on the phone in this damn stupid hospital.... I am sick of the smell of Lysol ... I could die of it.... I am sick of going to bed and I am sick of waking up.... I am tired ... I am tired of the truth ... and I am tired of lying about the truth ... I am tired of my skin.... I WANT OUT!

ORDERLY (*after a short pause*). Why don't you go into emergency ... and lie down?

(*He approaches her.*)

NURSE. Keep away from me.

(*At this moment the outside door bursts open and* JACK *plunges into the room. He is all these things: drunk, shocked, frightened. His face should be cut, but no longer bleeding. His clothes should be dirtied ... and in some disarray. He pauses, a few steps into the room, breathing hard.*)

Whoa! Hold on there, you.

ORDERLY (*not advancing*). What do you want?

JACK (*after more hard breathing; confused*). What ... ?

NURSE. You come banging in through that door like that? What's the matter with you? (*to the* ORDERLY) Go see what's the matter with him.

ORDERLY (*advancing slightly*). What do you *want*?

JACK (*very confused*). What do I want ... ?

ORDERLY (*backing off*). You can't come in here like this ... banging your way in here ... don't you know any better?

NURSE. You drunk?

JACK (*taken aback by the irrelevance*). I've been drinking ...

91

yes ... all right ... I'm drunk. (*intense*) I got someone outside ...

NURSE. You stop that yelling. This is a white hospital, you.

ORDERLY (*nearer the* NURSE). That's right. She's right. This is a private hospital ... a semi-private hospital. If you go on ... into the city ...

JACK (*shakes his head*). No....

NURSE. Now you listen to me, and you get this straight ... (*Pauses just perceptibly, then says the word, but with no special emphasis.*) ... nigger ... this is a semi-private white hospital ...

JACK (*defiant*). I don't care!

NURSE. Well, you *get* on....

ORDERLY (*as the* INTERN *re-enters with two containers of coffee*). You go on now ... you go ...

INTERN. What's all this about?

ORDERLY. I told him to go on into Memphis ...

INTERN. Be quiet. (*to* JACK) What is all this about?

JACK. Please ... I got a woman ...

NURSE. You been told to move on.

INTERN. You got a woman ...

JACK. Outside ... in the car.... There was an accident ... there is blood.... Her arm ...

(*The* INTERN, *after thinking for a moment, looking at the* NURSE, *moves towards the outside door.*)

INTERN. All right ... we'll go see. (*to the* ORDERLY, *who hangs back*) Come on, you ... let's go.

ORDERLY (*looks to the* NURSE). We told him to go on into Memphis.

NURSE (*to the* INTERN, *her eyes narrowing*). Don't you go out there!

INTERN (*ignoring her; to the* ORDERLY). You heard me ... come on!

NURSE (*strong*). I told you ... DON'T GO OUT THERE!

INTERN (*softly*, *sadly*). Honey ... you going to fix me? You going to have the mayor throw me out of here on my butt? Or are you going to arrange it in Washington to have me *deported*? What *are* you going to do ... hunh?

NURSE (*between her teeth*). Don't go out there....

INTERN. Well, honey, whatever it is you're going to do ... it might as well be now as any other time.

(*He and the* ORDERLY *move to the outside door.*)

NURSE (*half angry, half plaintive, as they exit*). Don't go!

(*After they exit*)

I warn you! I *will* fix you. You go out that door ... you're through here.

(JACK *moves to a vacant area near the bench, stage-right. The* NURSE *lights a cigarette.*)

I told you I'd fix you ... I'll fix you. (*now, to* JACK) I think I said this was a white hospital.

JACK (*wearily*). I know, lady ... you told me.

NURSE (*her attention on the door*). You don't have sense enough to do what you're told ... you make trouble for yourself ... you make trouble for other people.

JACK (*sighing*). I don't care....

NURSE. You'll care!

JACK (*softly, shaking his head*). No ... I won't care. (*now, half to her, half to himself*) We were driving along ... not very fast ... I don't think we were driving fast ... we were in a hurry, yes ... and I had been drinking ... *we* had been drinking ... but I *don't* think we were driving fast ... not too fast ...

NURSE (*her speeches now are soft comments on his*). ... driving drunk on the road ... it not even dark yet ...

JACK. ... but then there was a car ... I hadn't seen it ... it couldn't have seen me ... from a side road ... hard, fast, sudden ... (*Stiffens.*) ... CRASH! (*Loosens.*) ... and we weren't thrown ... both of us ... both cars stayed on the road ... but we were stopped ... my motor, running.... I turned it off ... the door ... the right door was all smashed in.... That's all it was ... no more damage than that ... but we had been riding along ... laughing ... it was cool driving, but it was warm out ... and she had her arm out the window ...

NURSE. ... serves you right ... drinking on the road ...

JACK. ... and I said ... I said, Honey, we have crashed ... you all right? (*His face contorts.*) And I looked ... and the door was all pushed in ... she was caught there ... where the door had pushed in ... her right side, crushed into the torn door, the door crushed into her right side. ... BESSIE! BESSIE! ... (*more to the* NURSE, *now*) ... but ma'am ... her arm ... her right arm ... was torn off ... almost torn off from her shoulder ... and there was blood ... SHE WAS BLEEDING SO ... !

NURSE (*from a distance*). Like water from a faucet ... ? Oh, that is terrible ... terrible....

JACK. I didn't wait for nothin' ... the other people ... the other car ... I started up ... I started ...

NURSE (*more alert*). You took *off*? ... You took off from an accident?

JACK. Her arm, ma'am ...

NURSE. You probably got police looking for you right now ... you know that?

JACK. Yes, ma'am ... I suppose so ... and I drove ... there was a hospital about a mile up ...

NURSE (*snapping to attention*). THERE! You went somewhere *else*? You been somewhere else already? What are you doing *here* with that woman then, hunh?

JACK. At the hospital ... I came in to the desk and I told them what had happened ... and they said, you sit down and

wait ... you go over there and sit down and wait a while.
WAIT! It was a white hospital, ma'am ...

NURSE. *This* is a white hospital, too.

JACK. I said ... this is an emergency ... there has been an
accident.... YOU WAIT! You just sit down and wait....
I told them ... I told them it was an emergency ... I said ...
this woman is badly hurt ... YOU COOL YOUR HEELS!
... I said, Ma'am, I got Bessie Smith out in that car there....
I DON'T CARE WHO YOU GOT OUT THERE,
NIGGER ... YOU COOL YOUR HEELS! ... I couldn't
wait there ... her in the car ... so I left there ... I drove on
... I stopped on the road and I was told where to come ...
and I came here.

NURSE (*numb, distant*). I know who she is ... I heard her sing.
(*abruptly*) You give me your name! You can't take off
from an accident like that ... I'll phone the police; I'll
tell them where you are!

(*The* INTERN *and the* ORDERLY *re-enter. Their uniforms are
bloodied. The* ORDERLY *moves stage-rear, avoiding* JACK.
The INTERN *moves in, staring at* JACK.)

He drove away from an accident ... he just took off ... and
he didn't come right here, either ... he's been to one
hospital *already*. I *warned* you not to get mixed up in
this....

INTERN (*softly*). Shut up!

(*Moves toward* JACK, *stops in front of him.*)

You tell me something ...

NURSE. I warned you! You didn't listen to me ...

JACK. You want my name, too ... is that what you want?

INTERN. No, that's not what I want.

(*He is contained, but there is a violent emotion inside him.*)

You tell me something. When you brought her here ...

JACK. I brought her here.... They wouldn't help her....

INTERN. All right. When you brought her here ... when you brought this woman *here* ...

NURSE. Oh, this is no plain woman ... this is no ordinary nigger ... this is Bessie Smith!

INTERN. When you brought this woman *here* ... when you drove up *here* ... when you brought this woman *here* ... DID YOU KNOW SHE WAS DEAD?
    (*Pause.*)

NURSE. Dead! ... This nigger brought a dead woman here?

INTERN (*afraid of the answer*). Well ... ?

NURSE (*distantly*). Dead ... dead.

JACK (*wearily; turning, moving towards the outside door*). Yes ... I knew she was dead. She died on the way here.

NURSE (*snapping to*). Where you going? Where do you think you're going? I'm going to get the police here for you!

JACK (*at the door*). Just outside.

INTERN (*as* JACK *exits*). WHAT DID YOU EXPECT *ME* TO DO, EH? WHAT WAS *I* SUPPOSED TO *DO*?
    (JACK *pauses for a moment, looks at him blankly, closes the door behind him.*)

TELL ME! WHAT WAS I SUPPOSED TO DO?

NURSE (*slyly*). Maybe ... maybe he thought you'd bring her back to life ... great white doctor. (*Her laughter begins now, mounts to hysteria.*) Great ... white ... doctor.... Where are you going to go now ... great ... white ... doctor? You are finished. You have had your last patient here.... Off you go, boy! You have had your last patient ... a nigger ... a dead nigger lady ... WHO SINGS. Well ... I sing, too, boy ... I sing real good. You want to hear me sing? Hunh? You want to hear the way I sing? HUNH?
    (*Here she begins to sing and laugh at the same time. The singing is tuneless, almost keening, and the laughter is almost crying.*)

INTERN (*moves to her*). Stop that! Stop that!
>   (*But she can't. Finally he slaps her hard across the face. She is frozen, with her hand to her face where he hit her. He backs towards the rear door.*)

ORDERLY (*his back to the wall*). I never heard of such a thing ... bringing a dead woman here like that.... I don't know what people can be thinking of sometimes....
>   (*The* INTERN *exits. The room fades into silhouette again.... The great sunset blazes; music up.*)

CURTAIN

THE SANDBOX (1959)

A Brief Play, in Memory of my Grandmother (1876–1959)

Music by William Flanagan

FIRST PERFORMANCE: April 15th, 1960. New York City. The Jazz Gallery.

THE SANDBOX

The Players:

THE YOUNG MAN ...... 25.	A good-looking, well-built boy in a bathing suit.
MOMMY .... 55.	A well-dressed, imposing woman.
DADDY .... 60.	A small man; grey, thin.
GRANDMA .... 86.	A tiny, wizened woman with bright eyes.
THE MUSICIAN	No particular age, but young would be nice.

When, in the course of the play, MOMMY and DADDY call each other by these names, there should be no suggestion of regionalism. These names are of empty affection and point up the pre-senility and vacuity of their characters.

A bare stage, with only the following: Near the footlights, far stage-right, two simple chairs set side by side facing the audience; near the footlights, far stage-left, a chair facing stage-right with a music stand before it; farther back, and stage-centre, slightly elevated and raked, a large child's sandbox with a toy pail and shovel; the background is the sky, which alters from the brightest day to deepest night.

    At the beginning, it is brightest day; the YOUNG MAN *is alone on stage, to the rear of the sandbox, and to one side. He is doing callisthenics; he does callisthenics until quite at the very end of the play. These callisthenics, employing the arms only, should suggest the beating and fluttering of wings. The* YOUNG MAN *is, after all, the Angel of Death.*

MOMMY *and* DADDY *enter from stage-left,* MOMMY *first.*

MOMMY (*motioning to* DADDY). Well, here we are; this is the beach.

DADDY (*whining*). I'm cold.

MOMMY (*dismissing him with a little laugh*). Don't be silly; it's as warm as toast. Look at that nice young man over there: *he* doesn't think it's cold. (*Waves to the* YOUNG MAN.) Hello.

YOUNG MAN (*with an endearing smile*). Hi!

MOMMY (*looking about*). This will do perfectly ... don't you think so, Daddy? There's sand there ... and the water beyond. What do you think, Daddy?

DADDY (*vaguely*). Whatever you say, Mommy.

MOMMY (*with the same little laugh*). Well, of course ... whatever I say. Then, it's settled, is it?

DADDY (*shrugs*). She's *your* mother, not mine.

MOMMY. *I* know she's my mother. What do you take me for? (*A pause.*) All right, now; let's get on with it. (*She shouts into the wings, stage-left.*) You! Out there! You can come in now.

(*The* MUSICIAN *enters, seats himself in the chair, stage-left, places music on the music stand, is ready to play.* MOMMY *nods approvingly.*)

Very nice; very nice. Are you ready, Daddy? Let's go get Grandma.

DADDY. Whatever you say, Mommy.

MOMMY (*leading the way out, stage-left*). Of course, whatever I say. (*to the* MUSICIAN) You can begin now.

(*The* MUSICIAN *begins playing;* MOMMY *and* DADDY *exit;*

the MUSICIAN, *all the while playing, nods to the* YOUNG
MAN.)

YOUNG MAN (*with the same endearing smile*). Hi!

(*After a moment,* MOMMY *and* DADDY *re-enter, carrying*
GRANDMA. *She is borne in by their hands under her armpits;*
she is quite rigid; her legs are drawn up; her feet do not touch
the ground; the expression on her ancient face is that of
puzzlement and fear.)

DADDY. Where do we put her?

MOMMY (*the same little laugh*). Wherever I say, of course. Let me
see ... well ... all right, over there ... in the sandbox.
(*Pause.*) Well, what are you waiting for, Daddy? ... The
sandbox!

(*Together they carry* GRANDMA *over to the sandbox and*
more or less dump her in.)

GRANDMA (*righting herself to a sitting position; her voice a cross*
between a baby's laugh and cry). Ahhhhhh! Graaaaa!

DADDY (*dusting himself*). What do we do now?

MOMMY (*to the* MUSICIAN). You can stop now.

(*The* MUSICIAN *stops.*)

(*back to* DADDY) What do you mean, what do we do now?
We go over there and sit down, of course. (*to the* YOUNG
MAN) Hello there.

YOUNG MAN (*again smiling*). Hi!

(MOMMY *and* DADDY *move to the chairs, stage-right,*
and sit down. A pause.)

GRANDMA (*same as before*). Ahhhhhh! Ah-haaaaaa! Graaaaaa!

DADDY. Do you think ... do you think she's ... comfortable?

MOMMY (*impatiently*). How would I know?

DADDY (*pause*). What do we do now?

MOMMY (*as if remembering*). We ... wait. We ... sit here ... and
we wait ... that's what we do.

DADDY (*after a pause*). Shall we talk to each other?

MOMMY (*with that little laugh; picking something off her dress*). Well, *you* can talk, if you want to ... if you can think of anything to *say* ... if you can think of anything *new*.

DADDY (*thinks*). No ... I suppose not.

MOMMY (*with a triumphant laugh*). Of course not!

GRANDMA (*banging the toy shovel against the pail*). Haaaaaa! Ah-haaaaaa!

MOMMY (*out over the audience*). Be quiet, Grandma ... just be quiet, and wait.

(GRANDMA *throws a shovelful of sand at* MOMMY.)

(*still out over the audience*) She's throwing sand at me! You stop that, Grandma; you stop throwing sand at Mommy! (*to* DADDY) She's throwing sand at me.

(DADDY *looks around at* GRANDMA, *who screams at him.*)

GRANDMA. GRAAAAAA!

MOMMY. Don't look at her. Just ... sit here ... be very still ... and wait. (*to the* MUSICIAN) You ... uh ... you go ahead and do whatever it is you do.

(*The* MUSICIAN *plays.*

MOMMY *and* DADDY *are fixed, staring out beyond the audience.* GRANDMA *looks at them, looks at the* MUSICIAN, *looks at the sandbox, throws down the shovel.*)

GRANDMA. Ah-haaaaaa! Graaaaaa! (*Looks for reaction; gets none. Now ... directly to the audience —*) Honestly! What a way to treat an old woman! Drag her out of the house ... stick her in a car ... bring her out here from the city ... dump her in a pile of sand ... and leave her here to set. I'm eighty-six years old! I was married when I was seventeen. To a farmer. He died when I was thirty. (*to the* MUSICIAN) Will you stop that, please?

(*The* MUSICIAN *stops playing.*)

I'm a feeble old woman ... how do you expect anybody to hear me over that peep! peep! peep! (*to herself*) There's no respect around here. (*to the* YOUNG MAN) There's no respect around here!

YOUNG MAN (*same smile*). Hi!

GRANDMA (*after a pause, a mild double-take, continues, to the audience*). My husband died when I was thirty (*indicates* MOMMY), and I had to raise that big cow over there all by my lonesome. You can imagine what *that* was like. Lordy! (*to the* YOUNG MAN) Where'd they get *you*?

YOUNG MAN. Oh ... I've been around for a while.

GRANDMA. I'll bet you have! Heh, heh, heh. Will you look at you!

YOUNG MAN (*flexing his muscles*). Isn't that something? (*Continues his callisthenics.*)

GRANDMA. Boy, oh boy; I'll say. Pretty good.

YOUNG MAN (*sweetly*). I'll say.

GRANDMA. Where ya from?

YOUNG MAN. Southern California.

GRANDMA (*nodding*). Figgers; figgers. What's your name, honey?

YOUNG MAN. I don't know....

GRANDMA (*to the audience*). Bright, too!

YOUNG MAN. I mean ... I mean, they haven't given me one yet ... the studio ...

GRANDMA (*giving him the once-over*). You don't say ... you don't say. Well ... uh, I've got to talk some more ... don't you go 'way.

YOUNG MAN. Oh, no.

GRANDMA (*turning her attention back to the audience*). Fine; fine. (*then, once more, back to the* YOUNG MAN) You're ... you're an actor, hunh?

YOUNG MAN (*beaming*). Yes. I am.

GRANDMA (*to the audience again; shrugs*). I'm smart that way. *Anyhow*, I had to raise ... *that* over there all by my lonesome; and what's next to her there ... that's what she married. Rich? I tell you ... money, money, money. They took me off the *farm* ... which was real decent of them ... and they moved me into the big town house with *them* ... fixed a nice place for me under the stove ... gave me an army blanket ... and my own dish ... my very own dish! So, what have I got to complain about? Nothing, of course. I'm not complaining. (*She looks up at the sky, shouts to someone off stage.*) Shouldn't it be getting dark now, dear?

(*The lights dim; night comes on. The* MUSICIAN *begins to play; it becomes deepest night. There are spots on all the players, including the* YOUNG MAN, *who is, of course, continuing his callisthenics.*)

DADDY (*stirring*). It's night-time.

MOMMY. Shhhh. Be still ... wait.

DADDY (*whining*). It's so hot.

MOMMY. Shhhhhh. Be still ... wait.

GRANDMA (*to herself*). That's better. Night. (*to the* MUSICIAN) Honey, do you play all through this part?

(*The* MUSICIAN *nods.*)

Well, keep it nice and soft; that's a good boy.

(*The* MUSICIAN *nods again; plays softly.*)

That's nice.

(*There is an off-stage rumble.*)

DADDY (*starting*). What was that?

MOMMY (*beginning to weep*). It was nothing.

DADDY. It was ... it was ... thunder ... or a wave breaking ... or something.

MOMMY (*whispering, through her tears*). It was an off-stage rumble ... and you know what *that* means....

DADDY. I forget....

MOMMY (*barely able to talk*). It means the time has come for poor Grandma ... and I can't bear it!

DADDY (*vacantly*). I ... I suppose you've got to be brave.

GRANDMA (*mocking*). That's right, kid; be brave. You'll bear up; you'll get over it.

(*Another off-stage rumble ... louder.*)

MOMMY. Ohhhhhhhhhh ... poor Grandma ... poor Grandma....

GRANDMA (*to* MOMMY). I'm fine! I'm all right! It hasn't happened yet!

(*A violent off-stage rumble. All the lights go out, save the spot on the* YOUNG MAN; *the* MUSICIAN *stops playing.*)

MOMMY. Ohhhhhhhhhh.... Ohhhhhhhhhh....

(*Silence.*)

GRANDMA. Don't put the lights up yet ... I'm not ready; I'm not quite ready. (*Silence.*) All right, dear ... I'm about done.

(*The lights come up again, to brightest day; the* MUSICIAN *begins to play.* GRANDMA *is discovered, still in the sandbox, lying on her side, propped up on an elbow, half covered, busily shovelling sand over herself.*)

(*muttering*) I don't know how I'm supposed to do anything with this goddam toy shovel....

DADDY. Mommy! It's daylight!

MOMMY (*brightly*). So it is! Well! Our long night is over. We must put away our tears, take off our mourning ... and face the future. It's our duty.

GRANDMA (*still shovelling; mimicking*).... take off our mourning ... face the future.... Lordy!

(MOMMY *and* DADDY *rise, stretch.* MOMMY *waves to the* YOUNG MAN.)

YOUNG MAN (*with that smile*). Hi!

(GRANDMA *plays dead.* (!) MOMMY *and* DADDY *go over to look at her; she is a little more than half buried in the sand; the toy shovel is in her hands, which are crossed on her breast.*)

MOMMY (*before the sandbox; shaking her head*). Lovely! It's ...

it's hard to be sad ... she looks ... so happy. (*with pride and conviction*) It pays to do things well. (*to the* MUSICIAN) All right, you can stop now, if you want to. I mean, stay around for a swim, or something; it's all right with us. (*She sighs heavily.*) Well, Daddy ... off we go.

DADDY. Brave Mommy!

MOMMY. Brave Daddy!

(*They exit, stage-left.*)

GRANDMA (*after they leave; lying quite still*). It pays to do things well.... Boy, oh boy! (*She tries to sit up —*) ... well, kids ... (— *but she finds she can't.*) ... I ... I can't get up. I ... I can't move....

(*The* YOUNG MAN *stops his callisthenics, nods to the* MUSICIAN, *walks over to* GRANDMA, *kneels down by the sandbox.*)

I ... can't move....

YOUNG MAN. Shhhhh ... be very still....

GRANDMA. I ... I can't move....

YOUNG MAN. Uh ... ma'am; I ... I have a line here.

GRANDMA. Oh, I'm sorry, sweetie; you go right ahead.

YOUNG MAN. I am ... uh ...

GRANDMA. Take your time, dear.

YOUNG MAN (*prepares; delivers the line like a real amateur*). I am the Angel of Death. I am ... uh ... I am come for you.

GRANDMA. What ... wha ... (*then, with resignation —*) ... ohhhh ... ohhhh, I see.

(*The* YOUNG MAN *bends over, kisses* GRANDMA *gently on the forehead.*)

(GRANDMA, *her eyes closed, her hands folded on her breast again, the shovel between her hands, a sweet smile on her face*). Well ... that was very nice, dear....

YOUNG MAN (*still kneeling*). Shhhhhh ... be still....

GRANDMA. What I meant was ... you did that very well, dear....

YOUNG MAN (*blushing*). ... oh ...

GRANDMA. No; I mean it. You've got that ... you've got a quality.

YOUNG MAN (*with his endearing smile*). Oh ... thank you; thank you very much ... ma'am.

GRANDMA (*slowly; softly — as the* YOUNG MAN *puts his hands on top of hers*). You're ... you're welcome ... dear.

(*Tableau. The* MUSICIAN *continues to play as the curtain slowly comes down.*)

CURTAIN

THE ZOO STORY

A Play in One Scene (1958)

for
WILLIAM FLANAGAN

FIRST PERFORMANCE: September 28th, 1959. Berlin, Germany.
Schiller Theater Werkstatt.

THE ZOO STORY

The Players:

PETER: A man in his early forties, neither fat nor gaunt, neither handsome nor homely. He wears tweeds, smokes a pipe, carries horn-rimmed glasses. Although he is moving into middle age, his dress and his manner would suggest a man younger.

JERRY: A man in his late thirties, not poorly dressed, but carelessly. What was once a trim and lightly muscled body has begun to go to fat; and while he is no longer handsome, it is evident that he once was. His fall from physical grace should not suggest debauchery; he has, to come closest to it, a great weariness.

It is Central Park; a Sunday afternoon in summer; the present. There are two park benches, one towards either side of the stage; they both face the audience. Behind them: foliage, trees, sky. At the beginning, PETER is seated on one of the benches.

As the curtain rises, PETER is seated on the bench stage-right. He is reading a book. He stops reading, cleans his glasses, goes back to reading. JERRY enters.

JERRY. I've been to the zoo. (PETER *doesn't notice.*) I said, I've been to the zoo. MISTER, I'VE BEEN TO THE ZOO!

PETER. Hm? ... What? ... I'm sorry, were you talking to me?

JERRY. I went to the zoo, and then I walked until I came here. Have I been walking north?

PETER (*puzzled*). North? Why ... I ... I think so. Let me see.

JERRY (*pointing past the audience*). Is that Fifth Avenue?

PETER. Why yes; yes, it is.

JERRY. And what is that cross street there; that one, to the right?

PETER. That? Oh, that's Seventy-fourth Street.

JERRY. And the zoo is around Sixty-fifth Street; so, I've been walking north.

PETER (*anxious to get back to his reading*). Yes: it would seem so.

JERRY. Good old north.

PETER (*lightly, by reflex*). Ha, ha.

JERRY (*after a slight pause*). But not due north.

PETER. I … well, no, not due north; but, we … call it north. It's northerly.

JERRY (*watches as* PETER, *anxious to dismiss him, prepares his pipe*). Well, boy; *you're* not going to get lung cancer, are you?

PETER (*looks up, a little annoyed, then smiles*). No, sir. Not from this.

JERRY. No, sir. What you'll probably get is cancer of the mouth, and then you'll have to wear one of those things Freud wore after they took one whole side of his jaw away. What do they call those things?

PETER (*uncomfortable*). A prosthesis?

JERRY. The very thing! A prosthesis. You're an educated man, aren't you? Are you a doctor?

PETER. Oh, no; no. I read about it somewhere: *Time* magazine, I think. (*He turns to his book.*)

JERRY. Well, *Time* magazine isn't for blockheads.

PETER. No, I suppose not.

JERRY (*after a pause*). Boy, I'm glad that's Fifth Avenue there.

PETER (*vaguely*). Yes.

JERRY. I don't like the west side of the park much.

PETER. Oh? (*then, slightly wary, but interested*) Why?

JERRY (*off-hand*). I don't know.

PETER. Oh. (*He returns to his book.*)

JERRY (*stands for a few seconds, looking at* PETER, *who finally looks up again, puzzled*). Do you mind if we talk?

PETER (*obviously minding*). Why ... no, no.

JERRY. Yes you do; you do.

PETER (*puts his book down, his pipe out and away, smiling*). No, really; I don't mind.

JERRY. Yes you do.

PETER (*finally decided*). No; I don't mind at all, really.

JERRY. It's ... it's a nice day.

PETER (*stares unnecessarily at the sky*). Yes. Yes, it is; lovely.

JERRY. I've been to the zoo.

PETER. Yes, I think you said so ... didn't you?

JERRY. You'll read about it in the papers tomorrow, if you don't see it on your TV tonight. You have TV, haven't you?

PETER. Why yes, we have two; one for the children.

JERRY. You're married!

PETER (*with pleased emphasis*). Why, certainly.

JERRY. It isn't a law, for God's sake.

PETER. No ... no, of course not.

JERRY. And you have a wife.

PETER (*bewildered by the seeming lack of communication*). Yes!

JERRY. And you have children.

PETER. Yes; two.

JERRY. Boys?

PETER. No, girls ... both girls.

JERRY. But you wanted boys.

PETER. Well ... naturally, every man wants a son, but ...

JERRY (*lightly mocking*). But that's the way the cookie crumbles?

PETER (*annoyed*). I wasn't going to say that.

JERRY. And you're not going to have any more kids, are you?

PETER (*a bit distantly*). No. No more. (*then back, and irksome*) Why did you say that? How would you know about that?

JERRY. The way you cross your legs, perhaps; something in the voice. Or maybe I'm just guessing. Is it your wife?

PETER (*furious*). That's none of your business! (*A silence.*) Do you understand? (JERRY *nods.* PETER *is quiet now.*) Well, you're right. We'll have no more children.

JERRY (*softly*). That *is* the way the cookie crumbles.

PETER (*forgiving*). Yes ... I guess so.

JERRY. Well, now; what else?

PETER. What were you saying about the zoo ... that I'd read about it, or see ... ?

JERRY. I'll tell you about it, soon. Do you mind if I ask you questions?

PETER. Oh, not really.

JERRY. I'll tell you why I do it; I don't talk to many people — except to say like: give me a beer, or where's the john, or what time does the feature go on, or keep your hands to yourself, buddy. You know — things like that.

PETER. I must say I don't ...

JERRY. But every once in a while I like to talk to somebody, really *talk*; like to get to know somebody, know all about him.

PETER (*lightly laughing, still a little uncomfortable*). And am I the guinea pig for today?

JERRY. On a sun-drenched Sunday afternoon like this? Who better than a nice married man with two daughters and ... uh ... a dog? (PETER *shakes his head.*) No? Two dogs. (PETER *shakes his head again.*) Hm. No dogs? (PETER *shakes his head, sadly.*) Oh, that's a shame. But you look like an animal man. CATS? (PETER *nods his head, ruefully.*) Cats! But, that can't be your idea. No, sir. Your wife and daughters? (PETER *nods his head.*) Is there anything else I should know?

PETER (*has to clear his throat*). There are ... there are two parakeets. One ... uh ... one for each of my daughters.

JERRY. Birds.

PETER. My daughters keep them in a cage in their bedroom.

JERRY. Do they carry disease? The birds.

PETER. I don't believe so.

JERRY. That's too bad. If they did you could set them loose in the house and the cats could eat them and die, maybe. (PETER *looks blank for a moment, then laughs.*) And what else? What do you do to support your enormous household?

PETER. I ... uh ... I have an executive position with a ... a small publishing house. We ... uh ... we publish text-books.

JERRY. That sounds nice; very nice. What do you make?

PETER (*still cheerful*). Now look here!

JERRY. Oh, come on.

PETER. Well, I make around eighteen thousand a year, but I don't carry more than forty dollars at any one time ... in case you're a ... a holdup man ... ha, ha, ha.

JERRY (*ignoring the above*). Where do you live? (PETER *is reluctant.*) Oh, look; I'm not going to rob you, and I'm not going to kidnap your parakeets, your cats, or your daughters.

PETER (*too loud*). I live between Lexington and Third Avenue, on Seventy-fourth Street.

JERRY. That wasn't so hard, was it?

PETER. I didn't mean to seem ... ah ... it's that you don't really carry on a conversation; you just ask questions. And I'm ... I'm normally ... uh ... reticent. Why do you just stand there?

JERRY. I'll start walking around in a little while, and eventually I'll sit down. (*recalling*) Wait until you see the expression on his face.

PETER. What? Whose face? Look here; is this something about the zoo?

JERRY (*distantly*). The what?

PETER. The zoo; the zoo. Something about the zoo.

JERRY. The zoo?

PETER. You've mentioned it several times.

JERRY (*still distant, but returning abruptly*). The zoo? Oh, yes; the zoo. I was there before I came here. I told you that. Say, what's the dividing line between upper-middle-middle-class and lower-upper-middle-class?

PETER. My dear fellow, I ...

JERRY. Don't my dear fellow me.

PETER (*unhappily*). Was I patronizing? I believe I was; I'm sorry. But, you see, your question about the classes bewildered me.

JERRY. And when you're bewildered you become patronizing?

PETER. I ... I don't express myself too well, sometimes. (*He attempts a joke on himself.*) I'm in publishing, not writing.

JERRY (*amused, but not at the humour*). So be it. The truth *is*: *I* was being patronizing.

PETER. Oh, now; you needn't say that.

(*It is at this point that* JERRY *may begin to move about the stage with slowly increasing determination and authority, but pacing himself, so that the long speech about the dog comes at the high point of the arc.*)

JERRY. All right. Who are your favourite writers? Baudelaire and J. P. Marquand?

PETER (*wary*). Well, I like a great many writers; I have a considerable ... catholicity of taste, if I may say so. Those two men are fine, each in his way. (*warming up*) Baudelaire, of course ... uh ... is by far the finer of the two, but Marquand has a place ... in our ... uh ... national ...

JERRY. Skip it.

PETER. I ... sorry.

JERRY. Do you know what I did before I went to the zoo today?
I walked all the way up Fifth Avenue from Washington
Square; all the way.

PETER. Oh; you live in the Village! (*This seems to enlighten*
PETER.)

JERRY. No, I don't. I took the subway down to the Village so I
could walk all the way up Fifth Avenue to the zoo. It's
one of those things a person has to do; sometimes a
person has to go a very long distance out of his way to
come back a short distance correctly.

PETER (*almost pouting*). Oh, I thought you lived in the Village.

JERRY. What were you trying to do? Make sense out of things?
Bring order? The old pigeonhole bit? Well, that's easy;
I'll tell you. I live in a four-storey brownstone rooming-
house on the upper West Side between Columbus Avenue
and Central Park West. I live on the top floor; rear; west.
It's a laughably small room, and one of my walls is made
of beaverboard; this beaverboard separates my room from
another laughably small room, so I assume that the two
rooms were once one room, a small room, but not neces-
sarily laughable. The room beyond my beaverboard wall
is occupied by a coloured queen who always keeps his door
open; well, not always but *always* when he's plucking his
eyebrows, which he does with Buddhist concentration.
This coloured queen has rotten teeth, which is rare, and he
has a Japanese kimono, which is also pretty rare; and he
wears this kimono to and from the john in the hall, which is
pretty frequent. I mean, he goes to the john a lot. He
never bothers me, and never brings anyone up to his
room. All he does is pluck his eyebrows, wear his kimono
and go to the john. Now, the two front rooms on my
floor are a little larger, I guess; but they're pretty small,

too. There's a Puerto Rican family in one of them, a husband, a wife, and some kids; I don't know how many. These people entertain a lot. And in the other front room, there's somebody living there, but I don't know who it is. I've never seen who it is. Never. Never ever.

PETER (*embarrassed*). Why ... why do you live there?

JERRY (*from a distance again*). I don't know.

PETER. It doesn't sound a very nice place ... where you live.

JERRY. Well, no; it isn't an apartment in the East Seventies. But, then again, I don't have one wife, two daughters, two cats and two parakeets. What I do have, I have toilet articles, a few clothes, a hot plate that I'm not supposed to have, a can opener, one that works with a key, you know: a knife, two forks, and two spoons, one small, one large; three plates, a cup, a saucer, a drinking glass, two picture frames, both empty, eight or nine books, a pack of pornographic playing-cards, regular deck, an old Western Union typewriter that prints nothing but capital letters, and a small strong-box without a lock which has in it ... what? Rocks! Some rocks ... sea-rounded rocks I picked up on the beach when I was a kid. Under which ... weighed down ... are some letters ... please letters ... please why don't you do this, and please when will you do that letters. And when letters, too. When will you write? When will you come? When? These letters are from more recent years.

PETER (*stares glumly at his shoes, then —*). About those two empty picture frames ... ?

JERRY. I don't see why they need any explanation at all. Isn't it clear? I don't have pictures of anyone to put in them.

PETER. Your parents ... perhaps ... a girl-friend ...

JERRY. You're a very sweet man, and you're possessed of a truly enviable innocence. But good old Mom and good old Pop are dead ... you know? ... I'm broken up about it, too ...

I mean really. BUT. That particular vaudeville act is playing the cloud circuit now, so I don't see how I can look at them, all neat and framed. Besides, or, rather, to be pointed about it, good old Mom walked out on good old Pop when I was ten and a half years old; she embarked on an adulterous turn of our southern states ... a journey of a year's duration ... and her most constant companion ... among others, among many others ... was a Mr Barleycorn. At least, that's what good old Pop told me after he went down ... came back ... brought her body north. We'd received the news between Christmas and New Year's, you see, that good old Mom had parted with the ghost in some dump in Alabama. And, without the ghost ... she was less welcome. I mean, what was she? A stiff ... a northern stiff. At any rate, good old Pop celebrated the New Year for an even two weeks and then slapped into the front of a somewhat moving city omnibus, which sort of cleaned things out family-wise. Well no; then there was Mom's sister, who was given neither to sin nor the consolations of the bottle. I moved in on her, and my memory of her is slight excepting I remember still that she did all things dourly: sleeping, eating, working, praying. She dropped dead on the stairs to her apartment, my apartment then, too, on the afternoon of my high school graduation. A terribly middle-European joke, if you ask me.

PETER. Oh, my; oh, my.

JERRY. Oh, your what? But that was a long time ago, and I have no feeling about any of it that I care to admit to myself. Perhaps you can see, though, why good old Mom and good old Pop are frameless. What's your name? Your first name?

PETER. I'm Peter.

JERRY. I'd forgotten to ask you. I'm Jerry.

PETER (*with a slight nervous laugh*). Hello, Jerry.

JERRY (*nods his hello*). And let's see now; what's the point of having a girl's picture, especially in two frames? I have two picture frames, you remember. I never see the pretty little ladies more than once, and most of them wouldn't be caught in the same room with a camera. It's odd, and I wonder if it's sad.

PETER. The girls?

JERRY. No. I wonder if it's sad that I never see the little ladies more than once. I've never been able to have sex with, or, how is it put? ... make love to anybody more than once. Once; that's it .... Oh, wait; for a week and a half, when I was fifteen ... and I hang my head in shame that puberty was late ... I was a h-o-m-o-s-e-x-u-a-l. I mean, I was queer ... (*very fast*) ... queer, queer, queer ... with bells ringing, banners snapping in the wind. And for those eleven days, I met at least twice a day with the park superintendent's son ... a Greek boy, whose birthday was the same as mine, except he was a year older. I think I was very much in love ... maybe just with sex. But that was the jazz of a very special hotel, wasn't it? And now; oh, do I love the little ladies; really, I love them. For about an hour.

PETER. Well, it seems perfectly simple to me....

JERRY (*angry*). Look! Are you going to tell me to get married and have parakeets?

PETER (*angry himself*). Forget the parakeets! And stay single if you want to. It's no business of mine. I didn't start this conversation in the ...

JERRY. All right, all right. I'm sorry. All right? You're not angry?

PETER (*laughing*). No, I'm not angry.

JERRY (*relieved*). Good. (*now back to his previous tone*) Interesting that you asked me about the picture frames. I would have thought that you would have asked me about the pornographic playing-cards.

PETER (*with a knowing smile*). Oh, I've seen those cards.

JERRY. That's not the point. (*Laughs.*) I suppose when you were a kid you and your pals passed them around, or you had a pack of your own.

PETER. Well, I guess a lot of us did.

JERRY. And you threw them away just before you got married.

PETER. Oh, now; look here. I didn't *need* anything like that when I got older.

JERRY. No?

PETER (*embarrassed*). I'd rather not talk about these things.

JERRY. So? Don't. Besides, I wasn't trying to plumb your post-adolescent sexual life and hard times; what I wanted to get at is the value difference between pornographic playing-cards when you're a kid, and pornographic playing-cards when you're older. It's that when you're a kid you use the cards as a substitute for a real experience, and when you're older you use real experience as a substitute for the fantasy. But I imagine you'd rather hear about what happened at the zoo.

PETER (*enthusiastic*). Oh, yes; the zoo. (*then awkward*) That is ... if you ...

JERRY. Let me tell you about why I went ... well, let me tell you some things. I've told you about the fourth floor of the rooming-house where I live. I think the rooms are better as you go down, floor by floor. I guess they are; I don't know. I don't know any of the people on the third and second floors. Oh, wait! I do know that there's a lady living on the third floor, in the front. I know because she cries all the time. Whenever I go out or come back in, whenever I

pass her door, I always hear her crying, muffled, but ...
very determined. Very determined indeed. But the one
I'm getting to, and all about the dog, is the landlady. I
don't like to use words that are too harsh in describing
people. I don't like to. But the landlady is a fat, ugly,
mean, stupid, unwashed, misanthropic, cheap, drunken
bag of garbage. And you may have noticed that I very
seldom use profanity, so I can't describe her as well as I
might.

PETER. You describe her ... vividly.

JERRY. Well, thanks. Anyway, she has a dog, and I will tell
you about the dog, and she and her dog are the gate-
keepers of my dwelling. The woman is bad enough; she
leans around in the entrance hall, spying to see that I don't
bring in things or people, and when she's had her mid-
afternoon pint of lemon-flavoured gin she always stops me
in the hall, and grabs ahold of my coat or my arm, and she
presses her disgusting body up against me to keep me in a
corner so she can talk to me. The smell of her body and
her breath ... you can't imagine it ... and somewhere,
somewhere in the back of that pea-sized brain of hers, an
organ developed just enough to let her eat, drink and emit,
she has some foul parody of sexual desire. And I, Peter, I
am the object of her sweaty lust.

PETER. That's disgusting. That's ... horrible.

JERRY. But I have found a way to keep her off. When she talks
to me, when she presses herself to my body and mumbles
about her room and how I should come there, I merely
say: but, Love; wasn't yesterday enough for you, and the
day before? Then she puzzles, she makes slits of her tiny
eyes, she sways a little, and then, Peter ... and it is at this
moment that I think I might be doing some good in that
tormented house ... a simple-minded smile begins to form

on her unthinkable face, and she giggles and groans as she thinks about yesterday and the day before; as she believes and relives what never happened. Then, she motions to that black monster of a dog she has, and she goes back to her room. And I am safe until our next meeting.

PETER. It's so ... unthinkable. I find it hard to believe that people such as that really *are*.

JERRY (*lightly mocking*). It's for reading about, isn't it?

PETER (*seriously*). Yes.

JERRY. And fact is better left to fiction. You're right, Peter. Well, what I have been meaning to tell you about is the dog; I shall, now.

PETER (*nervously*). Oh, yes; the dog.

JERRY. Don't go. You're not thinking of going, are you?

PETER. Well ... no, I don't think so.

JERRY (*as if to a child*). Because after I tell you about the dog, do you know what then? Then ... then I'll tell you about what happened at the zoo.

PETER (*laughing faintly*). You're ... you're full of stories, aren't you?

JERRY. You don't *have* to listen. Nobody is holding you here; remember that. Keep that in your mind.

PETER (*irritably*). I know that.

JERRY. You do? Good.

(*The following long speech, it seems to me, should be done with a great deal of action, to achieve a hypnotic effect on Peter, and on the audience too. Some specific actions have been suggested, but the director and the actor playing Jerry might best work it out for themselves.*)

ALL RIGHT. (*as if reading from a huge bill-board*) THE STORY OF JERRY AND THE DOG! (*natural again*) What I am going to tell you has something to do with how sometimes it's necessary to go a long distance out of the way in order to come back a short distance correctly; or, maybe I only think that it has something to do with that. But, it's why I went to the zoo today, and why I walked north ... northerly, rather ... until I came here. All right. The dog, I think I told you, is a black monster of a beast: an oversized head, tiny, tiny ears, and eyes ... bloodshot, infected, maybe; and a body you can see the ribs through the skin. The dog is black, all black; all black except for the bloodshot eyes, and ... yes ... and an open sore on its ... *right* forepaw; that is red, too. And, oh yes; the poor monster, and I do believe it's an old dog ... it's certainly a misused one ... almost always has an erection ... of sorts. That's red, too. And ... what else? ... oh, yes; there's a grey-yellow-white colour, too, when he bares his fangs. Like this: Grrrrrrr! Which is what he did when he saw me for the first time ... the day I moved in. I worried about that animal the very first minute I met him. Now, animals don't take to me like Saint Francis had birds hanging off him all the time. What I mean is: animals are indifferent to me ... like people (*He smiles slightly.*) ... most of the time. But this dog wasn't indifferent. From the very beginning he'd snarl and then go for me, to get one of my legs. Not like he was rabid, you know; he was sort of a stumbly dog, but he wasn't half-assed, either. It was a good, stumbly run; but I always got away. He got a piece of my trouser leg, look, you can see right here, where it's mended; he got that the second day I lived there; but, I kicked free and got upstairs fast, so that was that. (*Puzzles.*) I still don't know to this day how the other roomers manage it, but you know what I *think*: I think it had to do only with me. Cozy. So. Anyway, this went on for over a week, whenever I came in; but never when I went out. That's funny. Or, it *was* funny. I could

pack up and live in the street for all the dog cared. Well, I
thought about it up in my room one day, one of the times
after I'd bolted upstairs, and I made up my mind. I decided:
First, I'll kill the dog with kindness, and if that doesn't
work ... I'll just kill him. (PETER *winces*.) Don't react,
Peter; just listen. So, the next day I went out and bought
a bag of hamburgers, medium rare, no catsup, no onion;
and on the way home I threw away all the rolls and kept
just the meat.

(*Action for the following, perhaps.*)
When I got back to the rooming-house the dog was
waiting for me. I half opened the door that led into the
entrance hall, and there he was; waiting for me. It figures. I
went in, very cautiously, and I had the hamburgers, you
remember; I opened the bag, and I set the meat down about
twelve feet from where the dog was snarling at me. Like
so! He snarled; stopped snarling; sniffed; moved slowly;
then faster; then faster towards the meat. Well, when he
got to it he stopped, and he looked at me. I smiled; but
tentatively, you understand. He turned his face back to the
hamburgers, smelled, sniffed some more, and then ...
RRRAAAAGGGGGHHHH, like that ... he tore into
them. It was as if he had never eaten anything in his life
before, except like garbage. Which might very well have
been the truth. I don't think the landlady ever eats anything but garbage. But. He ate all the hamburgers, almost
all at once, making sounds in his throat like a woman.
Then, when he'd finished the meat, the hamburger, and
tried to eat the paper, too, he sat down and smiled. I think
he smiled; I know cats do. It was a very gratifying few
moments. Then, BAM, he snarled and made for me again.
He didn't get me this time, either. So, I got upstairs, and I
lay down on my bed and started to think about the dog

again. To be truthful, I was offended, and I was damn mad, too. It was six perfectly good hamburgers with not enough pork in them to make it disgusting. I was offended. But, after a while, I decided to try it for a few more days. If you think about it, this dog had what amounted to an antipathy towards me; really. And, I wondered if I mightn't overcome this antipathy. So, I tried it for five more days, but it was always the same: snarl, sniff; move; faster; stare; gobble; RAAGGGHHH; smile; snarl; BAM. Well, now; by this time Columbus Avenue was strewn with hamburger rolls and I was less offended than disgusted. So, I decided to kill the dog.

(PETER *raises a hand in protest.*)

Oh, don't be so alarmed, Peter; I didn't succeed. The day I tried to kill the dog I bought only one hamburger and what I thought was a murderous portion of rat poison. When I bought the hamburger I asked the man not to bother with the roll, all I wanted was the meat. I expected some reaction from him, like: we don't sell no hamburgers without rolls; or, wha' d'ya wanna do, eat it out'a ya han's? But no; he smiled benignly, wrapped up the hamburger in waxed paper, and said: A bite for ya pussycat? I wanted to say: No, not really; it's part of a plan to poison a dog I know. But, you can't say 'a dog I know' without sounding funny; so I said, a little too loud, I'm afraid, and too formally: YES, A BITE FOR MY PUSSYCAT. People looked up. It always happens when I try to simplify things; people look up. But that's neither hither nor thither. So. On my way back to the rooming-house, I kneaded the hamburger and the rat poison together between my hands, at that point feeling as much sadness as disgust. I opened the door to the entrance hall, and there the monster was, waiting to take the offering and then

jump me. Poor bastard; he never learned that the moment
he took to smile before he went for me gave me time
enough to get out of range. BUT, there he was; male-
volence with an erection, waiting. I put the poison patty
down, moved towards the stairs and watched. The poor
animal gobbled the food down as usual, smiled, which
made me almost sick, and then, BAM. But, I sprinted up
the stairs, as usual, and the dog didn't get me, as usual.
AND IT CAME TO PASS THAT THE BEAST WAS
DEATHLY ILL. I knew this because he no longer attended
me, and because the landlady sobered up. She stopped me
in the hall the same evening of the attempted murder and
confided the information that God had struck her puppy-
dog a surely fatal blow. She had forgotten her bewildered
lust, and her eyes were wide open for the first time. They
looked like the dog's eyes. She snivelled and implored me to
pray for the animal. I wanted to say to her: Madam, I
have myself to pray for, the coloured queen, the Puerto
Rican family, the person in the front room whom I've
never seen, the woman who cries deliberately behind her
closed door, and the rest of the people in all rooming-
houses, everywhere; besides, Madam, I don't understand
how to pray. But ... to simplify things ... I told her I
would pray. She looked up. She said that I was a liar, and
that I probably wanted the dog to die. I told her, and there
was so much truth here, that I didn't want the dog to die. I
didn't, and not just because I'd poisoned him. I'm afraid
that I must tell you I wanted the dog to live so that I could
see what our new relationship might come to.

(PETER *indicates his increasing displeasure and slowly
growing antagonism.*)

Please understand, Peter; that sort of thing is important.
You must believe me; it *is* important. We have to know the

effect of our actions. (*Another deep sigh.*) Well, anyway; the dog recovered. I have no idea why, unless he was a descendant of the puppy that guarded the gates of hell or some such resort. I'm not up on my mythology. (*He pronounces the word myth-o-*logy.) Are you?

(PETER *sets to thinking, but* JERRY *goes on.*)

At any rate, and you've missed the eight-thousand-dollar question, Peter; at any rate, the dog recovered his health and the landlady recovered her thirst, in no way altered by the bow-wow's deliverance. When I came home from a movie that was playing on Forty-second Street, a movie I'd seen, or one that was very much like one or several I'd seen, after the landlady told me puppykins was better, I was so hoping for the dog to be waiting for me. I was ... well, how would you put it ... enticed? ... fascinated? ... no, I don't think so ... heart-shatteringly anxious, that's it: I was heart-shatteringly anxious to confront my friend again.

(PETER *reacts scoffingly.*)

Yes, Peter; friend. That's the only word for it. I was heart-shatteringly et cetera to confront my doggy friend again. I came in the door and advanced, unafraid, to the centre of the entrance hall. The beast was there ... looking at me. And, you know, he looked better for his scrape with the nevermind. I stopped; I looked at him; he looked at me. I think ... I think we stayed a long time that way ... still, stone-statue ... just looking at one another. I looked more into his face than he looked into mine. I mean, I can concentrate longer at looking into a dog's face than a dog can concentrate at looking into mine, or into anybody else's face, for that matter. But during that twenty seconds or two hours that we looked into each other's face, we made contact. Now, here is what I had wanted to happen: I loved the dog now, and I wanted him to love me. I had tried to love, and I had tried to kill, and both had been unsuccessful by themselves. I hoped ... and I don't really know why I expected the dog to understand anything, much less my motivations ... I hoped that the dog would understand.

(PETER *seems to be hypnotized.*)

It's just ... it's just that ... (JERRY *is abnormally tense, now.*) ... it's just that if you can't deal with people, you have to make a start somewhere. WITH ANIMALS! (*much faster now, and like a conspirator*) Don't you see? A person has to have some way of dealing with SOMETHING. If not with people ... SOMETHING. With a bed, with a cockroach, with a mirror ... no, that's too hard, that's one of the last steps. With a cockroach, with a ... with a ... with a carpet, a roll of toilet paper ... no, not that, either ... that's a mirror, too; always check bleeding. You see how hard it is to find things? With a street corner, and too many lights, all colours reflecting on the oily-wet streets ... with a wisp of smoke, a wisp ... of smoke ... with ... with pornographic playing-cards, with a strong-box ... WITHOUT A LOCK ... with love, with vomiting, with crying, with fury because the pretty little ladies aren't pretty little ladies, with making money with your body which is an act of love and I could prove it, with howling because you're alive; with God. How about that? WITH GOD WHO IS A COLOURED QUEEN WHO WEARS A KIMONO AND PLUCKS HIS EYEBROWS, WHO IS A WOMAN WHO CRIES WITH DETERMINATION BEHIND HER CLOSED DOOR ... with God who, I'm told, turned his back on the whole thing some time ago ... with ... some day, with people. (JERRY *sighs the next word heavily.*) People. With an idea; a concept. And where better, where ever better in this humiliating excuse for a jail, where better to communicate one single, simple-minded idea than in an entrance hall? Where? It would be A START! Where better to make a beginning ... to understand and just possibly be understood ... a beginning of an understanding, than with ...

(*Here* JERRY *seems to fall into almost grotesque fatigue.*)

... than with A DOG. Just that; a dog.

(*Here there is a silence that might be prolonged for a moment or so; then* JERRY *wearily finishes his story.*)

A dog. It seemed like a perfectly sensible idea. Man is a dog's best friend, remember. So: the dog and I looked at each other. I longer than the dog. And what I saw then has been the same ever since. Whenever the dog and I see each other we both stop where we are. We regard each other with a mixture of sadness and suspicion, and then we feign indifference. We walk past each other safely; we have an understanding. It's very sad, but you'll have to admit that it is an understanding. We had made many attempts at contact, and we had failed. The dog has returned to garbage, and I to solitary but free passage. I have not returned. I mean to say, I have *gained* solitary free passage, if that much further loss can be said to be gain. I have learned that neither kindness nor cruelty by themselves, independent of each other, creates any effect beyond themselves; and I have learned that the two combined, together, at the same time, are the teaching emotion. And what is gained is loss. And what has been the result: the dog and I have attained a compromise; more of a bargain, really. We neither love nor hurt because we do not try to reach each other. And, *was* trying to feed the dog an act of love? And, perhaps, was the dog's attempt to bite me *not* an act of love? If we can so misunderstand, well then, why have we invented the word love in the first place?

(*There is silence.* JERRY *moves to* PETER's *bench and sits down beside him. This is the first time* JERRY *has sat down during the play.*)

The Story of Jerry and the Dog: the end.

(PETER *is silent.*)

Well, Peter? (JERRY *is suddenly cheerful.*) Well, Peter? Do you think I could sell that story to the *Reader's Digest* and make a couple of hundred bucks for *The Most Unforgettable Character I've Ever Met*? Huh?

(JERRY *is animated, but* PETER *is disturbed.*)

Oh, come on now, Peter; tell me what you think.

PETER (*numb*). I ... I don't understand what ... I don't think I ... (*now almost tearfully*) Why did you tell me all of this?

JERRY. Why not?

PETER. I DON'T UNDERSTAND!

JERRY (*furious, but whispering*). That's a lie.

PETER. No. No, it's not.

JERRY (*quietly*). I tried to explain it to you as I went along. I went slowly; it all has to do with ...

PETER. I DON'T WANT TO HEAR ANY MORE. I don't understand you, or your landlady, or her dog....

JERRY. *Her* dog! I thought it was my ... No. No, you're right. It *is* her dog. (*Looks at* PETER *intently, shaking his head.*) I don't know what I was thinking about; of course you don't understand. (*in a monotone, wearily*) I don't live in your block; I'm not married to two parakeets, or whatever your set-up is. I am a *permanent transient*, and my home is the sickening rooming-houses on the West Side of New York City, which is the greatest city in the world. Amen.

PETER. I'm ... I'm sorry; I didn't mean to ...

JERRY. Forget it. I suppose you don't quite know what to make of me, eh?

PETER (*a joke*). We get all kinds in publishing. (*Chuckles.*)

JERRY. You're a funny man. (*He forces a laugh.*) You know that?
You're a very ... a richly comic person.

PETER (*modestly, but amused*). Oh, now, not really. (*still chuckling*)

JERRY. Peter, do I annoy you, or confuse you?

PETER (*lightly*). Well, I must confess that this wasn't the kind of afternoon I'd anticipated.

JERRY. You mean, I'm not the gentleman you were expecting.

PETER. I wasn't expecting anybody.

JERRY. No, I don't imagine you were. But I'm here, and I'm not leaving.

PETER (*consulting his watch*). Well, you may not be, but I must be getting home soon.

JERRY. Oh, come on; stay a while longer.

PETER. I really should get home; you see ...

JERRY (*tickles PETER's ribs with his fingers*). Oh, come on.
> (PETER *is very ticklish; as* JERRY *continues to tickle him his voice becomes falsetto.*)

PETER. No, I ... OHHHHH! Don't do that. Stop, Stop. Ohhh, no, no.

JERRY. Oh, come on.

PETER (*as JERRY tickles*). Oh, hee, hee, hee. I must go. I ... hee, hee, hee. After all, stop, stop, hee, hee, hee, after all, the parakeets will be getting dinner ready soon. Hee, hee. And the cats are setting the table. Stop, stop, and, and ... (*He is beside himself now.*) ... and we're having ... hee, hee ... uh ... ho, ho, ho.
> (JERRY *stops tickling* PETER, *but the combination of the tickling and his own mad whimsy has* PETER *laughing almost hysterically. As his laughter continues, then subsides,* JERRY *watches him, with a curious fixed smile.*)

JERRY. Peter?

PETER. Oh, ha, ha, ha, ha, ha. What? What?

JERRY. Listen, now.

PETER. Oh, ho, ho. What ... what is it, Jerry? Oh, my.

JERRY (*mysteriously*). Peter, do you want to know what happened at the zoo?

PETER. Ah, ha, ha. The what? Oh, yes; the zoo. Oh, ho, ho. Well, I had my own zoo there for a moment with ... hee, hee, the parakeets getting dinner ready, and the ... ha, ha, whatever it was, the ...

JERRY (*calmly*). Yes, that was very funny, Peter. I wouldn't have expected it. But do you want to hear about what happened at the zoo, or not?

PETER. Yes. Yes, by all means; tell me what happened at the zoo. Oh, my. I don't know what happened to me.

JERRY. Now I'll let you in on what happened at the zoo; but first, I should tell you why I went to the zoo. I went to the zoo to find out more about the way people exist with animals, and the way animals exist with each other, and with people too. It probably wasn't a fair test, what with everyone separated by bars from everyone else, the animals for the most part from each other, and always the people from the animals. But, if it's a zoo, that's the way it is. (*He pokes* PETER *on the arm.*) Move over.

PETER (*friendly*). I'm sorry, haven't you enough room? (*He shifts a little.*)

JERRY (*smiling slightly*). Well, all the animals are there, and all the people are there, and it's Sunday and all the children are there. (*He pokes* PETER *again.*) Move over.

PETER (*patiently, still friendly*). All right.

(*He moves some more, and* JERRY *has all the room he might need.*)

JERRY. And it's a hot day, so all the stench is there, too, and all the balloon sellers, and all the ice-cream sellers, and all the seals are barking, and all the birds are screaming. (*Pokes* PETER *harder.*) Move over!

PETER (*beginning to be annoyed*). Look here, you have more than enough room! (*But he moves more, and is now fairly cramped at one end of the bench.*)

JERRY. And I am there, and it's feeding time at the lion's house, and the lion keeper comes into the lion cage, one of the lion cages, to feed one of the lions. (*Punches* PETER *on the arm, hard.*) MOVE OVER!

PETER (*very annoyed*). I can't move over any more, and stop hitting me. What's the matter with you?

JERRY. Do you want to hear the story? (*Punches* PETER's *arm again.*)

PETER (*flabbergasted*). I'm not so sure! I certainly don't want to be punched in the arm.

JERRY (*punches* PETER's *arm again*). Like that?

PETER. Stop it. What's the matter with you?

JERRY. I'm crazy, you bastard.

PETER. That isn't funny.

JERRY. Listen to me, Peter. I want this bench. You go sit on the bench over there, and if you're good I'll tell you the rest of the story.

PETER (*flustered*). But ... what ever for? What *is* the matter with you? Besides, I see no reason why I should give up this bench. I sit on this bench almost every Sunday afternoon, in good weather. It's secluded here; there's never anyone sitting here, so I have it all to myself.

JERRY (*softly*). Get off this bench, Peter; I want it.

PETER (*almost whining*). No.

JERRY. I said I want this bench, and I'm going to have it. Now get over there.

PETER. People can't have everything they want. You should know that; it's a rule; people can have some of the things they want, but they can't have everything.

JERRY (*laughs*). Imbecile! You're slow-witted!

PETER. Stop that!

JERRY. You're a vegetable! Go lie down on the ground.

PETER (*intense*). Now *you* listen to me. I've put up with you all
afternoon.

JERRY. Not really.

PETER. LONG ENOUGH. I've put up with you long enough.
I've listened to you because you seemed ... well, because I
thought you wanted to talk to somebody.

JERRY. You put things well; economically, and, yet ... oh,
what is the word I want to put justice to your ... JESUS,
you make me sick ... get off here and give me my bench.

PETER. MY BENCH!

JERRY (*pushes* PETER *almost, but not quite, off the bench*). Get out of
my sight.

PETER (*regaining his position*). God da ... mn you. That's
enough! I've had enough of you. I will not give up this
bench; you can't have it, and that's that. Now, go away.

   (JERRY *snorts but does not move.*)

Go away, I said.

   (JERRY *does not move.*)

Get away from here. If you don't move on ... you're a
bum ... that's what you are.... If you don't move on,
I'll get a policeman here and make you go.

   (JERRY *laughs, stays.*)

I warn you, I'll call a policeman.

JERRY (*softly*). You won't find a policeman around here;
they're all over on the west side of the park chasing fairies
down from trees or out of the bushes. That's all they do.
That's their function. So scream your head off; it won't
do you any good.

PETER. POLICE! I warn you, I'll have you arrested. POLICE!
(*Pause.*) I said POLICE! (*Pause.*) I feel ridiculous.

JERRY. You look ridiculous: a grown man screaming for the police on a bright Sunday afternoon in the park with nobody harming you. If a policeman *did* fill his quota and come sludging over this way he'd probably take you in as a nut.

PETER (*with disgust and impotence*). Great God, I just came here to read, and now you want me to give up the bench. You're mad.

JERRY. Hey, I got news for you, as they say. I'm on your precious bench, and you're never going to have it for yourself again.

PETER (*furious*). Look, you; get off my bench. I don't care if it makes any sense or not. I want this bench to myself; I want you OFF IT!

JERRY (*mocking*). Aw ... look who's mad.

PETER. GET OUT!

JERRY. No.

PETER. I WARN YOU!

JERRY. Do you know how ridiculous you look *now*?

PETER (*his fury and self-consciousness have possessed him*). It doesn't matter. (*He is almost crying.*) GET AWAY FROM MY BENCH!

JERRY. Why? You have everything in the world you want; you've told me about your home, and your family, and *your own* little zoo. You have everything, and now you want this bench. Are these the things men fight for? Tell me, Peter, is this bench, this iron and this wood, is this your honour? Is this the thing in the world you'd fight for? Can you think of anything more absurd?

PETER. Absurd? Look, I'm not going to talk to you about honour, or even try to explain it to you. Besides, it isn't a question of honour; but even if it were, you wouldn't understand.

JERRY (*contemptuously*). You don't even know what you're saying, do you? This is probably the first time in your life you've had anything more trying to face than changing your cats' toilet box. Stupid! Don't you have any idea, not even the slightest, what other people *need*?

PETER. Oh, boy, listen to you; well, you don't need this bench. That's for sure.

JERRY. Yes; yes, I do.

PETER (*quivering*). I've come here for years; I have hours of great pleasure, great satisfaction, right here. And that's important to a man. I'm a responsible person, and I'm a GROWN-UP. This is my bench, and you have no right to take it away from me.

JERRY. Fight for it, then. Defend yourself; defend your bench.

PETER. You've *pushed* me to it. Get up and fight.

JERRY. Like a man?

PETER (*still angry*). Yes, like a man, if you insist on mocking me even further.

JERRY. I'll have to give you credit for one thing: you *are* a vegetable, and a slightly near-sighted one, I think ...

PETER. THAT'S ENOUGH....

JERRY. ... but, you know, as they say on TV all the time — you know — and I mean this, Peter, you have a certain dignity; it surprises me....

PETER. STOP!

JERRY (*rises lazily*). Very well, Peter, we'll battle for the bench, but we're not evenly matched.

(*He takes out and clicks open an ugly-looking knife.*)

PETER (*suddenly awakening to the reality of the situation*). You *are* mad! You're stark raving mad! YOU'RE GOING TO KILL ME!

(*But before* PETER *has time to think what to do,* JERRY *tosses the knife at* PETER's *feet.*)

JERRY. There you go. Pick it up. You have the knife and we'll be more evenly matched.

PETER (*horrified*). No!

(JERRY *rushes over to* PETER, *grabs him by the collar;* PETER *rises; their faces almost touch.*)

JERRY. Now you pick up that knife and you fight with me. You fight for your self-respect; you fight for that god-damned bench.

PETER (*struggling*). No! Let ... let go of me! He ... Help!

JERRY (*slaps* PETER *on each 'fight'*). You fight, you miserable bastard; fight for that bench; fight for your parakeets; fight for your cats; fight for your two daughters; fight for your wife; fight for your manhood, you pathetic little vegetable. (*Spits in* PETER's *face.*) You couldn't even get your wife with a male child.

PETER (*breaks away, enraged*). It's a matter of genetics, not man-hood, you ... you monster.

(*He darts down, picks up the knife and backs off a little; breathing heavily.*)

I'll give you one last chance; get out of here and leave me alone!

(*He holds the knife with a firm arm, but far in front of him, not to attack, but to defend.*)

JERRY (*sighs heavily*). So be it!

(*With a rush he charges* PETER *and impales himself on the knife. Tableau: For just a moment, complete silence,* JERRY *impaled on the knife at the end of* PETER's *still firm arm. Then* PETER *screams, pulls away, leaving the knife in* JERRY. JERRY *is motionless, on point. Then he, too, screams, and it must be the sound of an infuriated and fatally wounded animal. With the knife in him, he stumbles back to the bench that* PETER *had vacated. He crumbles there, sitting, facing* PETER, *his eyes wide in agony, his mouth open.*)

THE ZOO STORY

PETER (*whispering*). Oh my God, oh my God, oh my God ...
> (PETER *repeats these words many times, very rapidly.*
> JERRY *is dying; but now his expression seems to change.*
> *His features relax, and while his voice varies, sometimes*
> *wrenched with pain, for the most part he seems removed from*
> *his dying. He smiles.*)

JERRY. Thank you, Peter. I mean that, now; thank you very much.
> (PETER's *mouth drops open. He cannot move; he is trans-*
> *fixed.*)

Oh, Peter, I was so afraid I'd drive you away. (*He laughs as best he can.*) You don't know how afraid I was you'd go away and leave me. And now I'll tell you what happened at the zoo. I think ... I think this is what happened at the zoo ... I think. I think that while I was at the zoo I decided that I would walk north ... northerly, rather ... until I found you ... or somebody ... and I decided that I would talk to you ... I would tell you things ... and things that I would tell you would ... Well, here we are. You see? Here we *are*. But ... I don't know ... could I have planned all this? No ... no, I couldn't have. But I think I did. And now I've told you what you wanted to know, haven't I? And now you know all about what happened at the zoo. And now you know what you'll see in your TV, and the face I told you about ... you remember ... the face I told you about ... my face, the face you see right now. Peter ... Peter? ... Peter ... thank you. I came unto you (*He laughs, so faintly.*) and you have comforted me. Dear Peter.

PETER (*almost fainting*). Oh my God!

JERRY. You'd better go now. Somebody might come by, and you don't want to be here when anyone comes.

PETER (*does not move, but begins to weep*). Oh my God, oh my God.

141

JERRY (*most faintly, now; he is very near death*). You won't be coming back here any more, Peter; you've been dispossessed. You've lost your bench, but you've defended your honour. And Peter, I'll tell you something now; you're not really a vegetable; it's all right, you're an animal. You're an animal, too. But you'd better hurry now, Peter. Hurry, you'd better go ... see?

(JERRY *takes a handkerchief and with great effort and pain wipes the knife handle clean of fingerprints.*)

Hurry away, Peter.

(PETER *begins to stagger away.*)

Wait ... wait, Peter. Take your book ... book. Right here ... beside me ... on your bench ... my bench, rather. Come ... take your book.

(PETER *starts for the book, but retreats.*)

Hurry ... Peter.

(PETER *rushes to the bench, grabs the book, retreats.*)

Very good, Peter ... very good. Now ... hurry away.

(PETER *hesitates for a moment, then flees, stage-left.*)

Hurry away .... (*His eyes are closed now.*) Hurry away, your parakeets are making the dinner ... the cats ... are setting the table ...

PETER (*off stage, a pitiful howl —*). OH MY GOD!

JERRY (*his eyes still closed, he shakes his head and speaks; a combination of scornful mimicry and supplication*). Oh ... my ... God.

(*He is dead.*)

CURTAIN